DEAR JUDAS

DEAR JUDAS

AND OTHER POEMS
BY ROBINSON
JEFFERS

Afterword by Robert J. Brophy

LIVERIGHT
New York   London

Published simultaneously in Canada by Penguin Books
Canada Ltd, 2801 John Street, Markham,
Ontario L3R 1B4
Printed in the United States of America.

Library of Congress Cataloging in Publication Data
Jeffers, Robinson, 1887–1962.
Dear Judas, and other poems.
I. Title.
PS3519.E27D4   1977   811'.5'2   76–56144

ISBN 0-87140-113-4

Liveright Publishing Corporation,
500 Fifth Avenue, New York, N.Y. 10110
W. W. Norton & Company Ltd.,
37 Great Russell Street, London WC1B 3NU

3 4 5 6 7 8 9 0

CONTENTS

DEAR JUDAS
AND OTHER
POEMS

DEAR JUDAS

THEY have all died and their souls are extinguished;
   three remnant images of three passions too violent to
   vanish
Still haunt the garden; they are nearly unfleshed of time:
   but if they were they would be eternal: they are fad-
   ing.
JESUS:
Cypresses warped by the weight of many hundreds of
   years, these trees like columns of knobbed stone
Are not the same; remote seedlings of those; it is sure that
   nineteen hundred years have gone down,
Still I revisit my ancient garden, under the round white
   stone that shines in the gulf of sky
And in vain, being dead, aches for annihilation, whitening
   the night.

Now the torches come up to take me.
Dear Judas be comforted at last. The smoky red flares
   and the scared faces, the servants, the priests
Are all — and even the bit of money under your cloak —
   imaginary, Judas. You and I remain yet,
Re-dreaming under the moon our passions: but all this play
   is played out and all these people have been dead
A forest of years. The kiss comes next. What, must I
   prompt you?

JUDAS: I know you are neither God nor God's son.
But you are *my God.* [*He kisses him.*]
[*The people with torches, and the other people imagined
by the speakers, may be thought of as represented by a few
maskers moving abstractedly in dumb show.*]
                                Take him, dog-priests. I have done
    the worst thing I can imagine. Oh yes: for the money.
JESUS:
His phantom face is like a flayed man's face. Dear Judas,
    turn, dream rather the lion-colored hills
And soft shores of the lake. The locusts I think chirp in
    the storm of sunlight. No: it's a shepherd
Flutes in the shade under that rock.
JUDAS: The shepherd is happy:
    but Oh happy happy rock.
I think the burly shepherd when he knifes a lamb
Has no thought of its pain; or if he passes along the road-
    side the masts of crucified robbers
The Romans have caught, and some look down and cry to
    him, from rattling throats in the dry wind, straining
Their hands and feet, it is only a show to gape at. Yet
    sometime his own pain will possess him. Oh happy
Happy rock.
JESUS: Since you must dream, dream on from there.
JUDAS: Why, now, what luck have the fishermen drawn
From their blue glaze? A multitude runs to the bank to
    meet the boat. My eyes dazzle in the driving
Dust of the sun: Oh, that new prophet.
[*He approaches Jesus again.*]   I smell the green-
    fringed water across the dust and the smell
Of clothes and sweat.
[*He moves about as if struggling in a crowd.*]
                                No; I can never attain to him.

[*10*]

JESUS: Whoever is overburdened,
  or hopeless, or wretched,
Or lies between the teeth of the world: let him come to
  me, I am able to save him.
JUDAS: Master: listen!
When I was a child, and ran errands for my father from
  my father's shop,
A little brown dog followed me home. I fed it and loved
  it for I was a lonely child, and found it
A nook under the counter to lie at nights. One day it
  trotted among the stalls of the butchers,
A cleaver was thrown, I carried it home bleeding in my
  arms. It could neither live nor die and I heard it
Moaning five days and I saw its eyes. Master I am neither
  sick nor poor nor heavy with sins,
But I am in prison of my pity; the moaning of men and
  beasts torments me; the pain is not my own pain
From which I come praying for deliverance.
JESUS: To other men I say *Be merciful,*
  to you alone
Be cruel. Life is not to be lived without some balance.
JUDAS: I knew that you
  had no power to save me.
JESUS: Come back,
For I have the power. Your name is Judas Iscariot, I
  have long known you. Dear Judas, does it make you
  glad
To see men joyful? To watch them feasting or laughing or
  fine with drunkenness?
JUDAS: Master: I don't know why,
But I am never joyful to see that. Certainly I'm not
  grieved; but the others' joy is not mine,
Only their pain. My heart is lonely; I groan for their
  pain.

[*11*]

JESUS: You have then only the night side of love.
Be with me Judas, and I will teach you to love by day
    and by night. Peter: this is Judas Iscariot.
John: this is Judas, he will be with us. He is not poor;
    and he is the son of a careful shopkeeper.
We need some one with wit to care for our pennies, they're
    always dripping away, and the little almsgivings,
So, Peter, give him the purse to carry. It is no burden.
    Come, children. Dear Judas, come.
[*Jesus and Judas walk together among the trees at the
back of the garden. A woman of fifty, tall and lean, with
a passion-worn proud Jewish face, is entering. She does
not see the others nor they her.*]
THE WOMAN:
Never look down, stone trees.
I am only a poor half-crazed old woman
That come and sit in the grove after dark,
Too old and poor for any one to do me harm.
It is true that I'm one
Who has known great and bitter occasions.
Oh garden that the glory from my body haunted,
The shining that came forth from between my thighs . . .
Is gone: past the flower and the fall
I sit and sing a cracked song.
[*She sits on a stone in the white moonlight.*]
I bid you fishermen mending brown nets
On the white sand,
I bid you beware of the net, fishermen.
You never can see it,
It flies through the white air and we all are snapped in it.
No, but look round you.
You see men walking and they seem to be free,
But look at the faces, they're caught.
There was never a man cut himself loose.

[*12*]

. . . That's true but comfortless.

[*She sits on the left; Jesus and Judas come forward on the right.*]

Nor dead in their graves are not free,
The mistletoe root-threads
In the wood of the oak of the earth
Are a net, are a net.

JESUS:
They're kind people in the quiet dwellings of Bethany.
    Their faces reflect
My Father's face.

JUDAS: Master. Master, we hear you sometimes
    say *our Father;* and at other times
You say *my Father.*

JESUS [*trembling*]: Do you dare?
Who appointed Iscariot . . . I am not angry, I see that
    you ask in honor, I will not hide my glory
From those I love. It is trumpeted by ten thousand in
    heaven. Yet even from my own heart in my youth
This terrible dark and shining mystery was hidden.
I learned that the carpenter was not my father. Ah, Judas,
    you're tender-hearted, you'd have pitied the torture
And dark and burning fire of my days then. What could
    I think? Not to impute against my own source
An impossible shame. . . . I loathed my life, I was taken
    in a net. It drove me into the desert mountains,
Where, after I had fasted beyond the moon's ring, until
    my spirit was fluttering to leave the body, I then
Remembered the prophecies and heard voices from heaven.
    When I returned I asked her, *Was God my father?*
She wept and answered that He was my father. Also
    when John in Jordan baptized me a voice declared it
In thunder from the clear sky. It was heard by many,
    though now they are scattered. . . . I blame my mother.

She sinned, hoarding her knowledge in her heart's treasury.
Truly the torment of those days of my ignorance
Never has healed.

JUDAS: Master, we know that you are God's son.
Master, you are changed; the warm happiness
Seems not to radiate from your face as before.

JESUS: I feel my
immeasurable height above men.
My heart is lonely. The sun has risen behind us; let us go on.

JUDAS: Our black shadows that move
Immeasurably stretched on the white road, they seem to
reach even to Jerusalem, trouble my soul.
I wonder whether the evil that we reject from our hearts
is not destroyed but goes blackening forth
To infest others?

JESUS: You are too scrupulous. Look how the
city among the beautiful awakening hills
Shines by itself in the morning clearness, a jewel washed
with new milk.

JUDAS: Son of God, let me go back.
I am not prepared. I dread the shining like the shining of
paradise.

[*Jesus goes on; Judas returns and sees the woman. He
takes a coin from the purse and drops it into her lap, and
says:*]
Why did you not cry out, mother,
To our Lord when he passed? He is altogether devoted to
saving the helpless.

THE WOMAN: Eh? Do you still have saviors?
This one does wisely to walk at night. The surest-caught
fish twists in the net and babbles to the others,
The cords cutting his gills, *I have come to save you.*

[*14*]

JUDAS: It is not night but
  the pearl of morning, and the savior
Is the son of God. [*The woman shudders and is silent.*]
                    I say that the living God is his father.
THE WOMAN: I have this
  comfort: we are caught in the net,
And the monsters of our sin are not our own monsters, but
  the cords drawing.
JUDAS: He has come to forgive sins,
Though they were monstrous.
THE WOMAN: This is the night after the day;
  black and silver dream the stark trees;
And now that some other woman is damned is nothing to
  me.
JUDAS: As if this
  withered beggar-woman
Were incarnate Night found sitting by the wayside, she
    throws ... you throw magical darkness over my eyes,
So that I seem standing at midnight in a dreary garden.
    Good God, if one remembers the future ...
That would be frightful.
THE WOMAN: Wee wanton brawler
Pommeling the breast,
Baby if it's shrunken,
Whose lips but yours?
I Night am your mother,
Grow tall, wee bird,
And watch your shadow
Pointing you home.
    Do you begin to remember the future? Then we
  must dream our dreams hastily.
Life grows transparent: what's left us but to light the
  torches of violence, to line it visible with fire?

[*15*]

But though you scream with pain, remember you're only
   a shadow.
[*She peers up at his face.*]
Stand into the moon. You are the one
Who wanted to be more merciful than mercy. Well, you
   shall go where the net draws you. I Night the Mother
Watching the bright abortions pour from my womb,
Gods, men, and the stars and Cæsar,
Receive them with kindness when they stream home.
Listen, Judas, for this is your dream. Your Lord has raised
A dead man out of the grave, a man who'd begun rotting.
   Came up when he called. This witnessed miracle
Flying on all winds in the city and suburbs, his name be-
   gins at length to be known widely and the people
Believe, they flock to hear him, his innocent heart is exalted:
   so that he dreams more than a prophet's
Glory: a great king's. His wisdom's not of this world. He
   says in his heart, "The city fills for the passover,
The people know me, and I shall go up in triumph and the
   trumpets will blow. When all the folk as one man
Rise in the shining honor of righteousness: the Romans will
   be ashamed and respect them, and the prophet-killer
Herod will flee. The power of the people, sudden and erect
   and resolute, I trust my people."
JUDAS: Dear Master,
Too many have made rebellions before: they are drowned
   in blood.
THE WOMAN: He tells
   you that this one will not be blotted,
Not with one drop, Jew's nor Roman's nor a slave's; we
   are many, they few; we shall be merciful; a kingdom
Of peace and mercy.
JUDAS [*turning from her, throwing out his hand to re-*

strain some imaginary person whom he sees as present]:
No, Peter. No! That was too cruel.

THE WOMAN: His dream skips over to an easier pity.
He cannot bear this progress up to Jerusalem.

JUDAS: Peter has flung a stone and
has broken the hawk's wing.
The trustful hawk that perched in the fig-tree: now it will
never again rejoice in the blowing air
And blue spaces, but trail pain till it starves. Its wound
saves many sparrows? I know it. Oh Simon
Well called the Stone: what a net of cruelty
Life gasps in, inextricably involved; so that I know not
what to pray for but annihilation
For a blessing on life. The bird's pain's nothing, though it
grinds in my heart; all the groaning world, Simon.
Flogged slaves and tortured criminals, and bitter deaths of
the innocent. Who created it? Who can endure it? Does
no one,
Not even our Lord, feel it all but I alone? My soul is dark
with images, and all are dreadful,
Sword, scourge and javelin, and the Roman gibbet,
Women dying horribly in hopeless birth-pangs, men dying
of thirst and hunger, the miners dying in the mines
Under the stinking torches, in summer by the Red Sea, con-
sumed with labor in the metal darkness;
And the ankles eaten with rust, and the blood-striped backs,
of the oars in a thousand galleys: it would be salvation
To think that I could willingly bear the suffering — if it
were possible — for all that lives, I alone:
I dare not think so.

THE WOMAN [*laughing*]: But Simon says that if you've
got a stone you wing the next bird, that's natural.

JUDAS:
Oh, hush. Our Lord is coming from the house.

[*17*]

It's morning again, how the world bathes in light; and all
the long clear shadows lying toward Jerusalem.
See there's the fig-tree ... no, I'll forget my griefs ... in-
numerably spreading his broad green hands
Sweet with their night-dew to the new day. Oh happy tree.
JESUS [*coming in from the left, speaking to those imag-*
ined beside him]:   Keep back the
people from me; I am faint
With the height within. Children, remember always that
dreams are deceivers. No one's exempt from dreaming,
Not even I. But all's fraud: fragments of thought
Fitting themselves together without a mind. It seemed to
me that I stood on a higher tower
Than any pier of those three that blot the tender blue above
Herod's palace. Oh, beyond conception
Exalted over the hills and the seas. But the tower swayed
— it means nothing: perhaps I slept
Having remembered the tower guilty of blood in Siloam —
tottered and waved all its wild height,
I felt the rushes of the air and heard the stones crumbling
... I will not cross my day of decision
With a dream's mind. Look how this fig-tree shakes his
banners above me. I came fasting from the house
And now I am hungry, there will be fruit among the broad
leaves. What, utterly barren? Let neither man
Nor bird henceforth eat of these boughs that have
failed me.
JUDAS: Do you wish,
Master, the beautiful tree were dead?
JESUS:
What is that to you?
JUDAS: Oh Master. Master, your face is sor-
rowful, your eyes are bitter. Let us go back
To Galilee where the days were all glad.

[*18*]

JESUS: Faint-hearted, Ah brittle-hearted
counselor, must one build power
On the dry twigs and stubble of such friends as you? I tell
you freely that to-day will see done
What was determined before the rock was laid down under
the towers of the mountains. This jewel of time
Laid in my hand, rejected once would be lost forever. All
greatness is a wrestling with time,
And one who has got the grip of his gaunt opponent, if he
lets go will not thrive, not again, but go down
And the dust cover him, sheet over sheet above his for-
gotten face, century on century. I feel
Signs in my soul and know my occasion. My soul is all
towers.
That idle dream was the human part's rebellion against the
divine: it is dreadful for the frail flesh
Born of a woman to serve the triumphant occasions of God.
The lightnings and pinnacles of my spirit
Cry out and call me: my Father is my trumpet: and the
people's eyes. Indeed it is strange: I am now so lifted
Toward God that I seem to myself, among all these press-
ing
Faces and voices, rather to walk alone in an ancient gar-
den, among dark trunks of stone trees
And patches of moon; imagining these things.
I can shake it off. [*He addresses the imagined people.*]
Listen and hear me. I have gone in the
past privately up to Jerusalem; but now
My sun has risen, the hour shines and beckons, my day has
come up. It is not forbidden you now to proclaim me
What your hearts know. I am called of my Father to lead
this people; I work my calling. It is not my desire
But even a bitterness to me to be called a king; yet to this
purpose I was born. What's kingdom to *me?*

[*19*]

To me that walked with God my Father before the foundation of the earth? I ruled the angels in heaven:
And now I have come to a little place to save a lost people.
What's kingdom to *me?* I seem to myself
Rather to walk alone in an old garden and watch the moon through the trees. You will proclaim me
King of the Jews in the city Jerusalem; and. I must take and build up the throne of David, and shepherd
The flocks of God.

(Friend, go to that man's house to whom you have spoken and fetch the colt he has ready:
I must now ride in triumph to the city.)

I will ride among you up to Jerusalem to be your King,
And all the streets and palaces will shout my coming. Yet listen and hear me. Herod will flee to Rome,
And Rome shall fall down, her discaptained soldiers
Run gaping and be flung on heaps: now I command you all to be utterly merciful in that high moment,
On the ridge of victory.
Let it be bloodless: let not one body be pierced, one soul made sorrowful. The people rise as one man,
And who shall stay them? but I am making a new thing in the world,
I am making a kingdom not built on blood, I am making a power weaponed with love not violence; a white
Dominion; a smokeless lamp; a pure light.
JUDAS: Alas my Master.
Oh listen to me! He cannot hear me.
His ears are full of the foolish cries of these poor people.
His eyes are utterly visionary,
His mind wild with its dream. He is leading them up to sudden bloody destruction.
JESUS: Farewell, farewell

[*20*]

Little friendly Bethany to which I shall never return
But crowned a king.
[*He passes on, and approaches the far side of the scene.*]
              You narrow and envious and philac-
    teried foreheads, Ah generation of vipers,
I tell you that if these people should dare be silent the very
    stones of the pavement would shout *Hosanna.*
[*Jesus goes out, followed by Judas.*]
THE WOMAN [*she stands up and says*]:
I am very tired, and the sun is burning. I must have fallen
    on slumber while I rested by the road,
I dreamed of hearing a many people go shouting through
    a dark garden. While I was the mother Night
Including them all.... But I am Mary, the wife of Joseph.
    I have come up as fast as I could,
In hope to see my son at this time. My son is a great
    prophet among our villages, and now
They tell me that even Jerusalem is crazy to hear him. I
    heard that he has gone up more like a king ...
I'm sure he'd not rise against government ... the people
    threw down their cloaks under the wheels of his
    chariot
To color the road with purple and softness, and long green
    palm-leaves. But I come here with terror in my heart
To be near his triumph. Oh, while his fame flourishes I'll
    never intrude, I'll see his face from far off,
And the dear masterful sweetness of his face. A few per-
    haps will know that I am his mother, but no one
Will hear me claim him ... though indeed I'm not a peasant,
    he needn't be ashamed ... but he's been lovely from
    boyhood,
Superior and born a leader, and such a power of discourse.
    I wouldn't, however, go up to find him;
I'll visit here with his friends in Bethany.

[*She stands at the edge of the scene, on the left.*]
                                              Oh: don't you
    know me? I am the mother of the man you love.
 And you are Lazarus whom he raised from the dead. Your
    face has never changed since.
[*She goes out of sight. The moon shines through the
cypress trees during a pause; and Judas comes in, from
the right.*]
JUDAS [*terribly agitated*]:
The glory is departed.
Oh, he has changed and changed. But I, what shall I do?
    His mind is dreadfully exalted and bitter,
And divided. I cannot understand what he suffers but I see
    what he does. He went up shining;
Whenever the people shouted the winning favor we used
    to adore was like a flame sweetened
With wine and honey in his face and motions. But when
    he had entered the city the people became silent,
Expecting something. Then we could see that he also ex-
    pected something.—— That never came; and his face
Darkened. He then went up to the temple. But I and two
    others held close beside him, babbling like children
About the sights of the city, glad to be fools if we could
    divert the gloom of his mind. I showed him
The huge stones of the walls and terraces: he suddenly
    turned,
Stopped on the stair, and lifting his two clenched hands
    toward heaven, he screamed in a voice not like his own
To those below him, but like the lake gulls in Galilee over
    the full fishing-boats:
"They'll all be broken! Look at these stones that are as
    long as two men and the thickness of a man's height,
Not one shall stand but go down, the giants of old, not one
    be left on another. I destroy. I destroy.

The temple and the temple treasures, the priests and the
gray rabbis. No man shall be saved but those that be-
lieve me
The son of God.... What do I say," he shouted ... "the
son is the Father's equal. I, here, am God.
But keep it secret awhile." He looked at the people as
though he hated them. We could do nothing. I remem-
bered
How hard he has grown toward suffering lately, and care-
less of the poor. When the woman came and poured
that perfume
Over his hair and his clothes, enough in value to have saved
many from misery, he was pleased and praised her.
He is changed indeed.
He entered the temple: then those that vend pigeons to
offer at the altar, and the poor hucksters that sell
The holy ribbons and trays of sweetmeats: the courts are
crowded at passover-time: they seemed to enrage him.
He said, "Go forth. You are making the house of prayer a
thieves' den." He twisted a whip out of hard cords
And drove them, and made a screaming riot in the tem-
ple.... So all the people were gathered to him again
To follow him, because they love destruction. He has found
the dreadful key to their hearts. One poor old man
Had fallen and cut his forehead on the brass edge of the
tray, and lay weeping among the crushed candies,
His white hair matted with watery blood.
We lifted him up. I cannot tell whether Jesus has gone
mad, or has indeed grown
Too near the power that makes falcons and lions, earth-
quakes and Rome, as much as the corn in the fields
And the breasts of mothers, and the happier birds. He is
terrible now. He has the shining power a few moments
And then stands brooding dumb, or suddenly through the

old sweetness a jet of poison. I have begged and
     prayed to him,
On my knees, with tears, to return down from the city. He
     looked across me with haggard eyes and answered
That he was God, and would never go down. But then I
     heard that he has begun to despair, for he said
"The sacrifice has come to the temple: not a bull nor a
     goat: but God
Himself to God. Perhaps my kingdom is not of this world."
     Instantly he stretched his neck and shouted:
"This world is nothing. It is dust and spittle. All those that
     trust me inherit eternal life and eternal
Delight: all those that reject me shall scream
In fires a world with no end."
*[Seeing one approaching from the right Judas moves to-
ward the left, and Jesus enters, addressing a crowd of
people imagined about him.]*
JESUS: Ah Jerusalem, Jerusalem,
How I'd have covered you with my wings and shielded you
     from my Father's anger. But now you shall see
For the cold priests' sake and the lying scribes' sake and
     the mocking rabble's,
The son of a woman but not a man come down like a moun-
     tain eagle above you cowering and strike
The great stones of your walls asunder with his heel and
     crush your towers under the soles of his feet
Until you are taught. If the people had been united the
     triumph would have been bloodless: but now, woe, woe,
The mother city, the great stones on the ancient hill. The
     moon shall be blood and the sun darkened
And the stars fall. I bring not peace but a sword; the
     brother shall hate the brother and the child his father.
The old walls must be pulled down before the founding

[*24*]

of the new, the field must be broken before the spring
sowing,
The old wood must be cut before the young forest.
[*He goes out among the trees.*]
JUDAS: They
gape and follow; he has found the dreadful key to
their hearts.
Now I see clearly my duty and destiny.
                              ... The passion is
past, the bitter drop has been drained, the veins
In my hands and about my heart seem light and empty. I
am like a ghost of one who did something
Ages ago, walking in a dead garden under the white of the
moon.
THE WOMAN [*coming in from the left*]:
                              You happy traveler
Coming down from the crowded city: what news of the
prophet Jesus? How do men hear him?
JUDAS: With fear
And fascination, like birds charmed by a serpent.
THE WOMAN: Ah. Great-
ness never escaped envy. A few
Must hate the man whom all love. Go down: he is well rid
of you.
JUDAS: I am one of those that love him more nearly
Than their own lives. He saved me from despair
The time when the cruelties that are done under the sky
and all the oppressions trampled me to madness.
He has come perhaps nearer to God than any prophet
before.
THE WOMAN: I, here, plain as I am,
Homely as I am, I am his mother.
[*Judas shudders and is silent.*]

Oh why will you not
look me in the eyes and why are you trembling?
Has evil come down? I know it is terrible to lead this
people. But tell me quickly all the worst you have.
I shall endure it. [*With pride.*] The mother of Jesus is
not a weak woman.
JUDAS: He is well. ... Oh, he is well, mother. ...
The people gather like sheep under the shadow of his
boughs; against the white burning noon, and death
On the dry hills. I have watched his white beauty
Above them like the mastlight over a boat, or the pilot of
a boat sailing far waters
Uncharted, no prow has furrowed before, the pale face
flecked with foam of danger and the constant eyes
Threading the rage of the storm, the hand among reefs
unknown steady on the helm. [*Miserably: to him-
self.*] That I am the reef
To wreck my captain! Should I tell her that!
[*Jesus comes in and stands sorrowfully on the right of
the scene.*]
THE WOMAN: Oh happy
friend: for he must love you if you love him so well:
And maybe you've even touched him from day to day,
serving his food or the like: what does he aim at,
Do you think? What can he reach and have rest?
JUDAS: Mother:
those that ascend the mountain toward God have none.
And whoever dares in the endless cross-waves of time pilot
the people,
Until misfortune wrecks him has none.
THE WOMAN: I thought ... I be-
lieved you loved him. What name are you called?
JUDAS: Judas.
THE WOMAN:

Your face was like an uncovered grave when you said "misfortune." I will send and . . . no, but go up myself
And warn him of you.
[*She crosses over toward Jesus, walking wearily; but stops humbly at a little distance from him.*]
JUDAS: Even before the
fact my face is like a sepulchre in honest eyes
And my name is abominable. That's now . . . that's my calling.
I have seen dread in my life. I have seen a crucified man:
I can't . . . He was a robber and murderer.
The black spread-eagle against the white cloud
Is cut in my mind past cure; strained basket ribs, and pale
clay mouth opening and closing in the air.
If Jesus should persist in Jerusalem, preaching destruction, rousing the looting street-people: I see
The future as bitter clearly as the unendurable memory:
the sudden Roman hand of suppression,
The machine squadrons, the screaming streets cleared:
And the Roman vengeance, all the roadside masted with
moaning crucifixions, from the city to Bethany.
Oh Jesus, I also love men.
[*Jesus, on the extreme right of the scene, speaks to those imagined about him. His mother stands waiting outside the circle.*]
JESUS: Whether you ought to pay
tribute to Cæsar? Whose name's on the coin? Cæsar's?
JUDAS:
I think I have never been able in all the gray and futile
of my life
To stop one tear or staunch one man's wound, but now I
am able. I'll say to the priests "Quietness is all.
Take him at night. I'm one of his men and I can lead you
to his bed." What harm can they do him, but keep him

Three or four days for the city peace and dismiss him?
He has made no insurrection till now (from hour to hour
    he may do it — who knows his mind? — to captain
A river of blood) they'll only keep him quiet and dismiss
    him home. There he'll not dream of towers,
But the sweet and passionate mind walk humbly. And he'll
    forgive me, he'll let me follow him, we'll walk together
In the white dust between the fig and the olive, as in the
    days that break my heart to remember.
[*He stands rapt in thought.*]
JESUS:
... And to God the things that are God's. Some of you
    know
That God is here. God dreamed a dream yesterday for
    Israel but you were afraid. It is not you
That reject God, it is God rejecting this people. I dreamed
    a dream for the lion of Judah but the lion's
Dwindled to a dog: it will not lick the wounds of freedom
    and victory; it will lick the scab of its mange
And snuffle for a bone under Cæsar's table. Therefore I
    have twitched the cloth of my kingdom out of your
    hands
To reach it westward: the Romans have courage and power
    and discipline and what have *you?* Hatred and memo-
    ries.
They have no love in their hearts but you have mere
    hatred. See, while I speak you are ready to stone
    me. ... Oh children,
Oh little sudden children, how can I help but love you? I
    am not turned
From one soul here. ... But take up your sick: I'll heal
    none at this time. It is not easy to have seen
Hope die in rags, and be the fool of a city.
[*To one who seems to speak to him privately.*]

My mother? I
have no mother. [*To the people.*]
Go home to your places.
[*Judas passes heavily across the scene to go out on the
right.*]
MARY:
It is I, Jesus. I've come all the tired way from
Nazareth.
JESUS: You have not done wisely.
MARY: Look there: the man
With the hollow face and the torn cloak: has turned against
you, Judas his name, intends to betray you.
JESUS:
They all betray me. No one is able to betray me. You stood
here listening,
Did you not see me use them at pleasure? Sting them with
words until the stones jumped in their hands,
And show the other side of my heart and conquer them?
MARY: No
man is great enough to stand where you stand.
Kings have paid guards for the ebbs of favor; they buy
faithfulness.
JESUS: No *man*. That is true. Poor withered rose,
Does that which God has touched fade?
MARY: I am indeed so
tired ... [*turning away from him: to herself*] Oh, if
his confidence
Lies there: then I am the one that betrays him, with the
lie that covered my sin. Never forgiven. [*To her son.*]
Oh come home,
Come home, Jesus,
From the fierce cowardly city and too many people. I
watched their faces, their eyes are shallow and
whetted

Like the eyes of mice, and they have no faith. Their
   fathers murdered the prophets. The lake fishermen
   need you,
The kindly villagers need you.

JESUS: I have not come up to re-
   turn. The city is my Father's city.

MARY: Yes; David
Throned here; but change ...

JESUS: Why does your mind flee
My Father's name as if it were a trap?

MARY: Oh, oh, is it *not*
   a trap? It is this ... it is this ... belief,
Has lifted you up to over-dream nature, and scorn danger
   and wisdom. Oh, it is secret. Be a prophet
But not lay claim ... Be a king if you can, but not to go
   mad.

JESUS: Woman, is it true or not, that the spirit
Of God shadowed you, and you were yet a virgin, and
   became my mother?

MARY [*weeping*]:   Oh, oh, it is secret.

JESUS: I kept it
Secret until I came to my power; I spoke of myself as the
   Son of Man, I told no one
Who was my Father, until this time was prepared of
   triumph.

MARY: Misery, to see your power and your ruin
Sprouting from the one root.

JESUS [*beginning to tremble*]:You wept like this before
   when I asked you: your eyes hiding from mine.
You'd almost persuade ... I've not wholly
The clear faith that I had. ... I am either a bastard or the
   son of God: who was my father?

MARY [*sinking down before him, writhing with sobs,
   mutters*]: Neither one!

[*30*]

The great stone on the road by Nazareth. [*Aloud.*] Oh
God, God.
The most high God..... No sin, not to the end of the
world, is ever forgiven.
JESUS [*stands looking down at her and trembling, and
says after a silence*]: It is enough.
Stand up. Whatever you'd answered, I'd not
Be weak enough to let go the faith that is the fountain
of my life. As to the sin you weep at,
I'll not know what it is: it's wholly forgiven. The son of
God has the power to forgive sins.
But go. Go quickly. I will never question you again, I will
never see you again. Judas, your news was
Means to betray me: yes, truly: natural: I've loved him
too. Mother, I hold the shining triumph
Here in my hand, the kingdom and the glory: I shall not
fail but conquer. Leave me! [*He turns from her with
a violent gesture and she creeps away.*] Out of this
. . . weakness . . .
To go and let the mind sprawl from its throne, in the
desert again, talking with demons in the morning
And counting the moonlights with white pebbles . . . there's
a black one for you my mother . . . until this flesh
Falls off, to fall starving across a wind-furrow between
the stone and the sand and find repose
This time in earnest, would be a weakness . . . not to re-
turn to.
The entertainments of demons
Between the flayed hills. "Look, I will give you all this
glory." What glory? A few bones scoured by the sand-
blast
After the desert birds have finished,
Because faith is dead.

Yet, Demon, I am the son of God. Not now in a desert, in
   a dark garden. Oh, as for these Jews,
They are taught from childhood to swallow absurd marvels
Without winking, what is that to me? They have no other
   glory now. The girls find a kind-hearted
Carpenter to patch the skiff with a scrap of marriage, or
   a cobbler to mend the leak in the shoe: common,
These years of the fall. The mystery remains though.
He must have been lovely . . . you daughters of Jerusalem
   that you stir not up nor awaken my love . . .
He is lovelier than the desert dawns. Three . . . four times
   in my life I have been one with our Father,
The night and the day, the dark seas and the little foun-
   tains, the sown and the desert, the morning star
And the mountains against morning and the mountain
   cedars, the sheep and the wolves, the Hebrews and
   the free nomads
That eat camels and worship a stone, and the sun cures
   them like salt into the marrow in the bones;
All, all, and times future and past
The hanging leaves on one tree: there is not a word nor a
   dream nor any way to declare his loveliness
Except to have felt and known, to have *been* the beauty.
   Even the cruelties and agonies that my poor Judas
Chokes on: were there in the net, shining. The hawk
   shone like the dove. Why, there it is! Exultation,
You stripped dupe? I have gathered my ruins.
Life after life, at the bottom of the pit comes exultation.
   I seem to remember so many nights?
In the smell of old cypresses in the garden darkness. And
   the means of power,
All clear and formed, like tangible symbols laid in my
   mind. Two thousand years are laid in my hands
Like grains of corn. Not for the power: Oh, more than

power, actual possession. To be with my people,
In their very hearts, a part of their being, inseparable
    from those that love me, more closely touching them
Than the cloth of the inner garment touches the flesh.
That this is tyrannous
I know, that it is love run to lust: but I will possess them.
The hawk shines like the dove. Oh, power
Bought at the price these hands and feet and all this body
    perishing in torture will pay is holy
Their minds love terror, their souls cry to be sacrificed
    for: pain's almost the God
Of doubtful men, who tremble expecting to endure it. Their
    cruelty sublimed. And I think the brute cross itself,
Hewn down to a gibbet now, has been worshiped; it stands
    yet for an idol of life and power in the dreaming
Soul of the world and the waters under humanity, whence
    floating again
It will fly up heaven, and heavy with triumphant blood and
    renewal, the very nails and the beams alive.
I saw my future when I was with God; but now at length
    in a flashing moment the means: I frightfully
Lifted up drawing all men to my feet: I go a stranger
    passage to a greater dominion,
More tyrannous, more terrible, more true, than Cæsar or
    any subduer of the earth before him has dared to
    dream of
In a dream on his bed, over the prostrate city, before the
    pale weary dawn
Creeps through his palace, through the purple fringes,
    between the polished agate pillars, to steal it away.
JUDAS [*coming in and approaching him*]:
Master, I have so longed to find you alone. I beseech you,
    Oh I adjure you, to come away from this city.

JESUS: You? Poor nerve of pity, is it so hard to do what you have to do?

JUDAS: For insurrection is blind madness, and would be punished bloodily, lives upon lives. You have said that you love men: you go about to destroy them. Oh, master, the poor drift of the street, with no weapons: have you *seen* soldiers?

JESUS: I have seen the angels of God. When a handful of my followers dare to lift up their hands against authority: that is the signal to call down to our van the shining hosts of God.

JUDAS: O master. Oh our master, turn from this!... I have been spying for you: I come from mingling with the priests and the priests' servants: they mean to arrest you. To imprison you: to-night perhaps. Ah, my Lord. My savior in the past. I will call you my God: I beseech you to leave this city to its own damnations. But do not you accept the guilt of the deaths of men. By torture: Rome nails them to crosses.

JESUS: You have always been without faith, and the sick fool of your pity.

JUDAS [*falling on his knees, clutching at Jesus' cloak*]: You *teach* mercy: be merciful. All I ask is that you come away and not force destruction. To let the people alone is the mercy: all stirring is death to them. [*He lets go the cloak.*] I know by heart that agate inflexible look in his eyes. There is no hope in this merciless man: I must do my office.

JESUS:

Needs must, poor Judas. But I am not merciless. Does brown agate

Being wrung flow drops like these? After you've done it, and seen the issue, Judas, you'll need consoling,

And find no comforter: but how can I comfort you now
   beforehand?
For if I could make you understand the death and the life
   your deed mothers, you'd never do it,
And twenty centuries to come go captainless, for lack of
   your deed. If it is required of you to die ignorant,
What is that to you? I tell you feelingly, it is the honor
   of all men living to be dupes of God
And serve not their own ends nor understandings but His,
   and so die. I that am more than a man
Know this and more, and serve and *am served.*
JUDAS: You are assuming the blood-guiltiness of perhaps
   a hundred lives forfeit in torment for rebellion; and
   not that alone: all the statutes and taxes screwed
   tighter afterwards on all the innocent. You that
   preached mercy! But I am able to prevent you. It is
   necessary for one man to be put under restraint, to
   save the people. . . . Oh my friend, my once master,
   my love forever: forgive me before the act!
JESUS:
Listen to me now, Judas, and remember.
Because I know your scrupulous heart, and I don't wish
   you to die despairing. There is not one creature,
Neither yourself nor anyone, nor a fly nor flung stone, but
   does exactly and fatally the thing
That it needs must; neither less nor more. This is the roots
   of forgiveness. This is our secret, Judas.
For the people's hearts are not scrupulous like yours, and
   if they heard it they'd run on license and die,
In the falling and splitting world, now that the sword and
   civilization and exile will break the sureties
And ungroove the lives. . . . "I bid you beware of the net,
   fishermen.

You see men walking and they seem to be free but look at
  the faces, they're caught.
There was never a man cut himself loose." An old song,
  Judas, humming in my head, the woman my mother
Used to sing by the lake shore: I fear now she's forgotten
  it. It meant the net of God's will. A song
That fountains power to the powerful, and to all, endur-
  ance. Suck on that when I'm gone.
    —But make haste, my poor friend, see the priests and
  settle with them. I warn you, the time runs short:
  to-morrow I intend to raise such a crested wave of the
  people as will sweep me to my kingdom and drown
  resistance. I shall draw all men to me: when I am
  lifted up.
[*Judas goes, in haste, with a gesture of despair.*]
JESUS:
Now my heart is faint, even in the midst of its exultation.
  It is well for the Greek artist
Shaping a stone to some form of beauty; he holds the plan
  in his mind and hews to it, and what falls off
Is not hurt, nor the block moans at the mallet. But I that
  am cutting the world to a new shape
And making a good and beautiful form, not of stone, un-
  imagined before, a new age ... Oh horrible, to carve
A child out of the shuddering breast and body of my
  mother! ... Why do I dream that? Because I said
That those who do my will are my mother? She'll cry too,
  that unlucky mother of my body: but others
Have seen their sons killed, it is not uncommon. My poor
  Judas
I fear will die, or but linger maimed in the heart and self-
  tormenting: did I forget now to tell him
That his name shall ride with mine down forests of ages?
  But that's vanity. Oh, I'm not innocent. The chisel

Of *my* carving cuts flesh and bleeds.
[*To the mutes who have entered:*]
You are here, my faithful? Judas has fallen off from us,
    poor fellow, he has gone over to lean on priests. Now
    keep watch for me to-night: did you bring swords as
    I bade you? Two hacked old blades — Oh, it's enough.
We must always be ready to offer a form of resistance,
    for a signal to my Father, who will send the angels.
[*He withdraws from the mutes.*]
For mild submission might appease them and lose me the
    cross: without that
The fierce future world would never kneel down to slake its
    lusts at my fountain. Only a crucified
God can fill the wolf bowels of Rome; only a torture high
    up in the air, and crossed beams, hang sovereign
When the blond savages exalt their kings; when the north
    moves, and the hairy-breasted north is unbound,
And Cæsar a mouse under the hooves of the horses. . . .
    Alas, poor dreamer,
Dreaming wildly because you must die. I know certainly
    the cross will conquer; but Rome to go down,
Or nations be born to colonize with new powers and
    peoples, and my gaunt pain erected in counterfeit,
The coasts of undreamed of oceans, is delirium.
[*He returns to the mutes, who seem to be asleep.*]
When I am bitterly troubled in spirit, could you not keep
    watch for me one hour?
[*He withdraws from the mutes.*]
The long obscure future like a weeping cloud covers me
    with sadness. Dear Judas, make haste!
Ere my heart fail and repent and renounce power. All
    power crushes its object, there is none innocent.
Religion is the most tyrannous, worming its way through
    the ears and eyes to the cup of the spirit, overgrowing

The life in its pool with alien and stronger life, drugging
    the water at the well-head: so I possess them
From inward: no man shall live
As if *I* had not lived. The hawk of my love is not left
    hungry. I sacrifice to this end all the hopes
Of these good villagers who've come up from Galilee ex-
    pecting kingdom; and the woman my mother; and my
    own
Flesh to be tortured; and my poor Judas, who'll do his
    office and break; and dreadful beyond these, un-
    numbered
Multitudes of souls from wombs unborn yet; the wasted
    valor of ten thousand martyrs: Oh, my own people
Perhaps will stab each other in a sacred madness, dis-
    puting over some chance word that my mouth made
While the mind slept. And men will imagine hells and go
    mad with terror, for so I have feathered the arrows
Of persuasion with fire, and men will put out the eyes of
    their minds, lest faith
Become impossible being looked at, and their souls perish.
                        . . . But what
    are men *now?*
Are the bodies free, or the minds full of clear light, or the
    hearts fearless? I having no foothold but slippery
Broken hearts and despairs, the world is so heaped against
    me, am yet lifting my peoples nearer
In emotion, and even at length in powers and perception,
    to the universal God than ever humanity
Has climbed before. . . . Dreams, dreams. Who can pick
    out the good from the evil? . . . It is likely that all
    these futures
Are only the raving mind of one about to be killed, myself
    and my poor Judas alone

Will bear the brunt; I shall go up and die and be pres-
ently forgotten. I have been deluded again,
Imagination my traitor, as often before. I am in the net,
and this deliberately sought
Torture on the cross is the only real thing.
                                        Yonder the
torches blink and dip among the black trunks.
They have lost the path, now they have found it again,
and up the stone steps.
                        Dear Judas, it is God drives us.
It is not shameful to be duped by God. I have known his
glory in my lifetime, I have *been* his glory, I know
Beyond illusion the enormous beauty of the torch in which
our agonies and all are particles of fire.
[*To his three or four companions, as the torches surround
him :*]
What, will you let them take me? Strike, Peter! He has
missed the head
And cut a man's ear: save yourselves! Enough's done
To edge the required judgment.
[*To the others:*]
Let my friends go. I am the one. Tell them so, Judas.
[*His companions escape among the trees. Jesus is led out
to the right, with Judas and the mutes of the other party.
A pause, Mary comes in from the left.*]
MARY:
They have brought me words that shine like new stars. . . .
Oh omnipotent God, with whom through delusion he
is joined in truth,
How marvelously thou hast made my secret sin the glory
of the world. I saw his triumph in his eyes
Before they told me. Without my sin he'd not have been
born, nor yet without my falsehood have triumphed,

For that exalted his deceived heart to the height of his
    destiny. Now they have told me that to-day
Is the set day, and he enters his kingdom. He will appear
    with those calm shining eyes before Herod,
And Herod will step down from his place and kneel down;
    and before Pontius Pilate the Roman governor,
Whose cold face will forget its pride. They both shall be
    dumb with shame, but Jesus will speak proudly
And kindly his decrees. I feared at first for a while, re-
    membering my sin, but now I am confident.
[*A mute passes.*]   Oh traveler,
What news, what news? Oh, I knew it!

                                         My soul doth mag-
    nify the Lord, who maketh light out of darkness,
Honor out of shame, out of sin a shining. I knew from the
    first day, from the lips finding the breast,
From the day when the babe looked in my face and smiled.
His hand puts down the mighty and exalts the humble. All
    generations shall call me blessed.
[*A mute passes.*]   Oh traveler,
What news, what news?

                        That is a lie, traveler. Lies glide
    about the city like fishes in a pool.
What the eyes have not seen is a lie. . . . Merciful God!
    whom I blasphemed in the bitter shame of his eyes:
But thou, Lord, knowest that my mind had gone wild with
    shame, and I was myself deceived at first, being igno-
    rant,
A child and a fool, and love had come to my soul in the
    holy evening, in the field, in the flush of twilight,
And I knew nothing . . .
Will no one come from the city and tell me? . . . I wish
    the night of darkness would cover me and I were
    asleep

[*40*]

Under deep waters, until the sandals of the man bearing
true tidings be heard in the dust.

[*She covers her eyes and sits erect, shuddering at mo-
ments, with her shawl drawn over her eyes. A cross is set
up, burdened with the form of a man, distantly visible at
the back of the scene. A mute passes in the foreground.*]

MARY:

What news, Oh what news?

                     ... You little gardens about
Bethany, did you hear this man? Oh mountains

And headlands of the north you have heard him; wide,
ribbed and waterless desert, Oh freedom of the Arab
horsemen

And sunrise and the lions: for his words are true.

He tells me plainly that my son is exalted as on a hill, and
uplifted on a high place,

The people of the city flocking to his feet. They feed on
the light of his face: he is called their king; he be-
holds them.

You leap you mountains like flames, Oh Lebanon the forest
shakes, you little round hills like lambs of the flock

Dancing and butting with the curly foreheads: but as for
me, I am stricken, I can neither speak nor be glad,

I require nothing but death; I suffered too much, just now,
while I was quiet, while I sat waiting,

Joy is a sword, like a sharp sword.

[*She sits stonily erect, with open eyes and the lifted hag-
gard features of ecstasy. A man with an unchangeable
bluish face enters and speaks without approaching Mary.*]

LAZARUS:

I am Lazarus who lay dead four days; and having known
death and the dreams of corruption and lived after-
wards

For several years, and again died, and rotted in the rock
   tomb, it is not possible for me
To be deluded like others by any of the habits of death. I
   also am only a shell and remainder
Like the other three ghosts that haunt the garden; but
   never subdued by their dreams, and being incapable
   of pity,
Astonishment or fear or any other of the accidents of life,
   I am sent every night at this time
To tell this woman not to rejoice; and that her son is
   condemned. It would be better for these three
If they could sleep; but the great passions life was not
   wide enough for are not so easily exhausted,
But echo in the wood for certain years or millenniums. As
   for myself, being wholly released from pain
And pleasure, sleeping and waking are all one.... This
   woman is so full-joyed at the false tidings her dream
Deludes her with, I would fain linger a little before
   I slay joy.
[*He stands about the center of the scene, rigidly repose-*
ful, and waits in silence.]
MARY: Lord God: prayer-hearing Lord,
Oh beautiful and loving God, I have one thing left to im-
   plore. Bless thou the traveler who passed but now
And brought me true word of my son's triumphs. His body
   and his soul, his house and his sons, be happy forever.
Add nothing to me. The straining crystal spirit and the
   broken old mother-body can hold no more
Happiness.
LAZARUS: Hail Mary, chosen for extremes. Remember
   that grief and happiness are only shadows of a shadow.
A blade of grass is a thing but these are not things,
And sooner withered.
MARY: Not a thing but a fire: my happiness

[*42*]

consumes me. Oh friend, you are not a stranger but Lazarus,
Whose guest I am: you have watched my son crowned
    king, and the winning favor of his ways when the
    people honored him.
Tell me nothing yet, for my heart is full.
LAZARUS: I would I might
    tell you nothing.
MARY: Oh why is your face not changed,
Lazarus, Lazarus?
LAZARUS: Come into the house; for what I have to
    say ought not to be said by the road,
Where those that pass may see you and stare at you, a
    chosen woman.
MARY: I will not stir from this place.
LAZARUS: It is possible for
Rumors not to be true.
MARY: Oh I know it, dear friend. I heard
    false tidings before the true came, and grieved
Before I was glad. . . . Your face not changed? I thought
    it would surely change when Jesus whom you love is
    glorified
In the favor of God and the great city. Yes, now I can see
Joy in your face.
LAZARUS: No, Mary, I am out of that net. I would
    to God that you were out of that net.
MARY:
You have always been strange, they say, since you were
    called from the cavern, with the hands and the face
    wrapped in white cloths.
. . . I am not so pierced with joy as I was: now you may
    tell me a little: a few of the words of Jesus
When he was praised; and whether he could keep from

weeping. *I* cannot. The tears keep trickling, whatever
I do.

LAZARUS:

He is not well.

MARY: Oh, I am sorry. It's one of the headaches he
suffers after long days of sun.

His spirit was always too hard a rider for the gentle body.

LAZARUS: Alas,
the crown that they crowned him with
Was painful; he endures anguish also in the hands
And in the feet; there were red stripes on his back. I think
he cannot live long.

MARY: How . . . stripes, Lazarus?
God help you, it is not your will to bring me false news,
but your mind is crazed
Since the rock tomb.

LAZARUS: My thoughts were made straight
there; and quieted, filled with the light of darkness.
The minds are crazed
That take joy at a penny's worth or pain at a penny's.

MARY: I have
my joy, you shall not frighten it away.

LAZARUS:

But while you are clutching it, while you speak of it, you
writhe with fear. Oh strong mother of one of the
greatest
Of torchlike men: there is only one pathway to peace for
a great passion. Truth is the way, take the truth
Against your breast and endure its horns. So life will at
last be conquered. After some thousands of years
The smoky unserviceable remainders of love and desire will
be dissolved and be still. . . . Your son
Has chosen his tools and made his own death; he has
chosen a painful death in order to become a God.

[*44*]

MARY:

Ah poor flawed mind: you'd make me think my Jesus as
    wise as yourself, would you?... Listen, Lazarus...
    you'll do well... go about the market-place singing
    riddles to people. Have a boy with a drum, and the
    half-caste Greeks will ring farthings on the drum-
    skin. You'll be the best juggler... that blue-dead face
    will fetch crowds, the resurrected man...
Where is he now, in the temple?

LAZARUS: He is hanged on a cross
    on the hill Golgotha.

MARY: Fool. To dream I'd believe...
This is for my sin, this false terror; and his triumphs for
    my love. It is hard that I am so choked with sickness,
A stone in my throat, when I must walk to the city. Ai,
    God. Why do men lie?

[*Judas enters from the right, accompanied by several
mutes. They are moving toward Lazarus and Mary.*]

JUDAS: ...Telling my reasons.
I am Judas running like a snapping dog along the streets
    of Jerusalem, snapping my reasons.
I say to one man:

[*He speaks to one of the mutes.*]

           Hear me, eyes! To get the firebrand
    locked up, to save the city. What we need is peace.
But who'd have dreamed they'd condemn him?

[*To another:*]   Money, money, money.
Now mercy's been made a fool and pity is a murderer,
What won't a man do for the fat silver? A pity that I
    threw it back to them...

[*To a third:*]

          I swear before God, friend,
I'm not the person that did it, I'm not... Let me go.

[*45*]

[*To Mary:*] Do y'
    see a brand, Madam,
On the mouth or brow? Am I marked? God marks them.
MARY [*to Lazarus*]: What
    is this creature?
JUDAS: That means innocent murderers: but me:
The person that kills his...
[*Looking at Lazarus:*] Bluebottle, don't I know you?
    And this one's... Oh!... This old woman
Is the cave it came from.
[*He falls on his knees before Mary, and tries to clutch
the skirt of her garment.*]
    I loved him, mother.
MARY [*to Lazarus*]: If it's a dog
    will you keep it off me? The slaver's poisonous
When they go mad. Oh: dead man:
He'd never be warned: I warned him: I knew this hollow
    and vile
Face from the first, when it said "misfortune." But Jesus,
    because I warned him of treachery, has walked into
    treachery.
I wish my mouth had been stopped with the seas of drown-
    ing.
[*She strikes at Judas' head with her hand.*]
    I don't believe. I don't believe. God's eyes
Are not put out yet, you are all liars. Oh! Oh! Oh!
LAZARUS: Cry out
    all your heart, Mary,
Because you believe: me, and the ball of repentance moan-
    ing here at your feet, and the witnesses here.
MARY:
When my eyes see it I'll believe and die.
[*Looking up; triumphantly:*] Look there where
    he comes, freely striding, angrily. Oh faithless.

Oh fools. You *wished* him to be dead.
                    . . . It is not he; I am cheated.
JUDAS: I remember my reason. Listen to me,
I have to tell you my reason: it was all for deliverance: I
    thought, by doing the worst imaginable thing
I should be freed of tormenting pity. Wasn't that . . .
    No. No.
MARY: You think, perhaps, kneeling there,
That I will curse you? Because you betrayed my son, be-
    cause you are infamous, because no viper is made
Venomous, nor reptile of the slime loathsome, to your
    measure? You think I'll be troubled for that? I'll
    stand here and pray
God to fill up your hollow face with fire for a lantern in
    hell? To bathe the long yellow fingers
In melted iron?
I will not curse you, Judas, I will curse myself. I am the
    first that betrayed him. The mothers, we do it:
Wolf-driven by love, or out of compliance, or fat conven-
    ience:
A child for Moloch. I am that woman: the giver of blood
    and milk to be sacrificed. I'll never tell you,
Though worse follows, how else I betrayed again
My blood and my milk. I built it up and forced it up and
    adored it, and the end's unbearable.
LAZARUS: Be silent.
Those inflamed, rolling and desert eyes, and the voice
    dragged through sand-colored lips, know nothing of
    the end.
You'd use a lonely and towered sorrow, and face the
    anguished core with cut stone, if you could feel
Fixed on you out of the dark the yearning innumerable
    eyes of many nations and an age of the world
Worshiping the mother of God, this palsied old woman.

[*47*]

Your son has done what men are not able to do;
He has chosen and made his own fate. The Roman Cæsar
    will call your son his master and his God; the floods
That wash away Cæsar and divide the booty, shall worship
    your son. The unconjectured selvages
And closed orbits of the ocean ends of the earth shall hear
    of him.
MARY: It was bitter enough when I was alone:
And now we are put into a pit to be stared at. I will go and
    find him.
[*She goes off toward the distantly seen cross.*]
JUDAS: There, there, slowly the Mother
Night: but I can hurry and run home to her; I ache for
    darkness.
LAZARUS: You, Judas, cease trembling. You were his
    tool
And broke to serve him: the power that makes the future
    so consumes the present. Therefore your name shall
    couple
With his in men's minds for many centuries: you enter
    his kingdom with him, as the hawk's lice with the
    hawk
Climb the blue towers of the sky under the down of the
    feathers.
JUDAS: If blue-face were as cunning as he looks
He'd know what I hide under my coat: look here: a noosed
    cord. What's that for? Find one for yourself, Lazarus,
And undo the cruellest miracle man ever suffered. I am go-
    ing a little distance into the wood
And buy myself an eternal peace for three minutes of
    breathlessness, never to see any more
The tortured nailed-up body in my mind, nor hear the use-
    less and endless moaning of beasts and men.

[*48*]

LAZARUS:

Let him go. He has done all he was made for; the rest's his
    own. Let him and the other at the poles of the wood,
Their pain drawn up to burning points and cut off, praise
    God after the monstrous manner of mankind.
While the white moon glides from this garden; the glory
    of darkness returns a moment, on the cliffs of dawn.

THE LOVING SHEPHERDESS

I

THE little one-room schoolhouse among the redwoods
Opened its door, a dozen children ran out
And saw on the narrow road between the dense trees
A person — a girl by the long light-colored hair:
The torn brown cloak that she wore might be a man's
Or woman's either — walking hastily northward
Among a huddle of sheep. Her thin young face
Seemed joyful, and lighted from inside, and formed
Too finely to be so wind-burnt. As she went forward
One or another of the trotting sheep would turn
Its head to look at her face, and one would press
Its matted shoulder against her moving thigh.
The schoolchildren stood laughing and shouting together.
"Who's that?" "Clare Walker," they said, "down from the
          hills.
She'd fifty sheep and now she's got eight, nine,
Ten: what have you done with all the others,
          Clare Walker?"
The joy that had lived in her face died, she yet
Went on as if she were deaf, with forward eyes
And lifted head, but the delicate lips moving.
The jeering children ran in behind her and the sheep
Drew nervously on before, except the old ram,
That close at her side dipped his coiled horns a little

But neither looked back nor edged forward. An urchin
    shouted
"You killed your daddy, why don't you kill your sheep?"
And a fat girl, "Oh where's your lover, Clare Walker?
He didn't want you after all."

                                 The patriarch ram
That walked beside her wore a greasy brown bundle
Tied on his back with cords in the felt of wool,
And one of the little boys, running by, snatched at it
So that it fell. Clare bent to gather it fallen,
And tears dropped from her eyes. She offered no threat
With the bent staff of rosy-barked madrone-wood
That lay in her hand, but said "Oh please, Oh please,"
As meek as one of her ewes. An eight-year-old girl
Shrilled, "Whistle for the dogs, make her run like a cat,
Call your dog, Charlie Geary!" But a brown-skinned
Spanish-Indian boy came forward and said,
"You let her alone. They'll not hurt you, Clare Walker.
Don't cry, I'll walk beside you." She thanked him,
    still crying.
Four of the children, who lived southward, turned back;
The rest followed more quietly.

                                 The black-haired boy
Said gently "Remember to keep in the road, Clare Walker.
There's enough grass. The ranchers will sick their dogs
    on you
If you go into the pastures, because their cows
Won't eat where the sheep have passed; but you can walk
Into the woods." She answered, "You're kind, you're kind.
Oh yes, I always remember." The small road dipped
Under the river when they'd come down the hill,
A shallow mountain river that Clare skipped over

By stone after stone, the sheep wading beside her.
The friendly boy went south to the farm on the hill, "good-
by, good-by," and Clare with her little flock
Kept northward among great trees like towers in the river-
valley. Her sheep sidled the path, sniffing
The bitter sorrel, lavender-flowering in shade, and the with-
ered ferns. Toward evening they found a hollow
Of autumn grass.

II

              Clare laughed and was glad, she undid
the bundle from the ram's back
And found in the folds a battered metal cup and a broken
loaf. She shared her bread with the sheep,
A morsel for each, and prettily laughing
Pushed down the reaching faces. "Piggies, eat grass. Leave
me the crust, Tiny, I can't eat grass.
Nosie, keep off. Here Frannie, here Frannie." One of the
ewes came close and stood to be milked, Clare stroked
The little udders and drank when the cup filled, and filled
it again and drank, dividing her crust
With the milch ewe; the flock wandered the glade, nibbling
white grass. There was only one lamb among them,
The others had died in the spring storm.

              The light in the glade suddenly
increased and changed, the hill
High eastward began to shine and be rosy-colored, and
bathed in so clear a light that up the bare hill
Each clump of yucca stood like a star, bristling sharp rays;
while westward the spires of the giant wood
Were strangely tall and intensely dark on the layered

colors of the winter sundown; their blunt points touched
The high tender blue, their heads were backed by the amber, the thick-branched columns
Crossed flaming rose. Then Clare with the flush
Of the solemn and glad sky on her face went lightly down to the river to wash her cup; and the flock
Fed on a moment before they looked up and missed her. The ewe called Frannie had gone with Clare and the others
Heard Frannie's hooves on the crisp oak-leaves at the edge of the glade. They followed, bleating, and found their mistress
On the brink of the stream, in the clear gloom of the wood, and nipped the cresses from the water. Thence all returning
Lay down together in the glade, but Clare among them
Sat combing her hair. with a gap-toothed comb brought from the bundle. The evening deepened, the thick blond strands
Hissed in the comb and glimmered in the brown twilight, Clare began weeping, full of sorrow for no reason
As she had been full of happiness before. She braided her hair and pillowed her head on the bundle; she heard
The sheep breathing about her and felt the warmth of their bodies, through the heavy fleeces.

                                    In the night she moaned
And bolted upright. "Oh come, come,
Come Fern, come Frannie, Leader and Saul and Tiny,
We have to go on," she whispered, sobbing with fear, and stood
With a glimmer in her hair among the sheep rising. The halved moon had arisen clear of the hill,

And touched her hair, and the hollow, in the mist from the
    river, was a lake of whiteness. Clare stood wreathed
    with her flock
And stared at the dark towers of the wood, the dream faded
    away from her mind, she sighed and fondled
The frightened foreheads. "Lie down, lie down darlings,
    we can't escape it." But after that they were restless
And heard noises in the night till dawn.

                          They rose in the quivering
Pale clearness before daylight, Clare milked her ewe,
The others feeding drifted across the glade
Like little clouds at sunrise wandering apart;
She lifted up the madrone-wood staff and called them.
"Fay, Fern, Oh Frannie. Come Saul.
Leader and Tiny and Nosie, we have to go on."
They went to the stream and then returned to the road
And very slowly went north, nibbling the margin
Bushes and grass, tracking the tender dust
With numberless prints of oblique crossings and driftings.
They came to Fogler's place and two ruffian dogs
Flew over the fence: Clare screaming "Oh, Oh, Oh, Oh,"
An inarticulate wildbird cry, brandishing
The staff but never striking, stood out against them,
That dashed by her, and the packed and trembling ball
Of fleeces rolling into the wood was broken.
The sheep might have been torn there, some ewe
    or the lamb
Against the great foundations of the trees, but Fogler
Ran shouting over the road after his dogs
And drove them home. Clare gathered her flock, the sobbing
Throats and the tired eyes, "Fay, Fern, Oh Frannie,
Come Leader, come little Hornie, come Saul;" and Fogler:
"You ought to get a good dog to help take care of them."

[54]

He eyed curiously her thin young face,
Pale parted lips cracked by the sun and wind,
And then the thin bare ankles and broken shoes.
"Are you Clare Walker? I heard that you'd gone away:
But you're Clare Walker, aren't you?" "We had a dog,"
She said, "a long time ago but he went away.
There, Nosie. Poor Frannie. There. These poor things
Can find their food, but what could I keep a dog with?
But that was some years ago." He said, "Are these all?
They're all gathered? I heard you'd thirty or forty."
Then hastily, for he saw the long hazel eyes
Filling with tears, "Where are you going, Clare Walker?
Because I think it will rain in a week or two,
You can't sleep out then." She answered with a little
    shudder,
"Wherever I go this winter will be all right.
I'm going somewhere next April." Fogler stood rubbing
His short black beard, then dropped his hand to scratch
The ram's forehead by the horns but Saul drew away.
And Fogler said: "You're too young and too pretty
To wander around the country like this.
I'd ask you to come here when it rains, but my wife . . .
And how could I keep the sheep here?" "Ah, no," she an-
    swered,
"I couldn't come back." "Well, wait," he said, "for a
    minute,
Until I go to the house. Will you wait, Clare?
I'll tie up the dogs. I've got some biscuit and things . . ."
He returned with a sack of food, and two old shoes
A little better than Clare's. She sat on a root;
He knelt before her, fumbling the knotted laces
Of those she had on, and she felt his hands tremble.
His wife's shoes were too short for the slender feet. When
    the others

Had been replaced, Fogler bent suddenly and kissed
Clare's knee, where the coat had slipped back. He looked
        at her face,
His own burning, but in hers nor fear nor laughter,
Nor desire nor aversion showed. He said "good-by,"
And hurried away.

                        Clare traveled northward, and sometimes
Half running, more often loitering, and the sheep fed.
In the afternoon she led them into the willows,
And choosing a green pool of the shallow stream
Bathed, while the sheep bleated to her from the shoals.
They made a pleasant picture, the girl and her friends, in
        the green shade
Shafted with golden light falling through the alder
        branches. Her body, the scare-crow garments laid by,
Though hermit-ribbed and with boyishly flattened flanks
        hardly a woman's,
Was smooth and flowing, glazed with bright water, the
        shoulders and breasts beautiful, and moved with a
        rapid confidence
That contradicted her mind's abstractions. She laughed
        aloud and jetted handfuls of shining water
At the sheep on the bank; the old ram stood blinking with
        pleasure, shaking his horns. But after a time Clare's
        mood
Was changed, as if she thought happiness must end.
She shivered and moved heavily out of the stream
And wept on the shore, her hands clasping her ankles,
Her face bowed on her knees, her knotted-up coils
Of citron-colored hair loosening. The ewe
That she called Nosie approached behind her and pressed
Her chin on the wet shoulder; Clare turned then, moaning,
And drew the bony head against the soft breasts.

"Oh what will you do," she whispered laughing
     and sobbing,
"When all this comes to an end?"

                              She stood and stroked off
The drops of water, and dressed hastily. They went
On farther; now there was no more forest by the road,
But open fields. The river bent suddenly westward
And made a pond that shone like a red coal
Against the shore of the ocean, under the sundown
Sky, with a skeleton of sand-bar
Between the pond and the sea.

                              When deepening twilight
Made all things gray and made trespass safe, Clare entered
The seaward fields with her flock. They had fed scantly
In the redwood forest, and here on the dead grass
The cattle had cropped all summer they could not sleep.
She led them hour after hour under the still stars.
Once they ran down to the glimmering beach to avoid
The herd and the range bull; they returned, and wandered
The low last bluff, where sparse grass labors to live in the
     wind-heaped sand. Silently they pastured northward,
Gray file of shadows, between the glimmer and hushing
     moan of the ocean and the dark silence of the hills.
The erect one wore a pallor of starlight woven in her hair.
     Before moonrise they huddled together
In a hollow cup of old dune that opened seaward, but shel-
     tered them from the nightwind and from morning eyes.

III

The bleating of sheep answered the barking of sea-lions
     and Clare awoke

Dazzled in the broad dawn. The land-wind lifted the light-
    spun manes of the waves, a drift of sea-lions
Swung in the surf and looked at the shore, sleek heads up-
    lifted and great brown eyes with a glaze of blind
Blue sea-light in them. "You lovely creatures," she whis-
    pered.
She went to the verge and felt the foam at her ankles. "You
    lovely creatures come closer." The sheep followed her
And stopped in the sand with lonesome cries. Clare stood
    and trembled at the simple morning of the world; there
    was nothing
But hills and sea, not a tree on the shore nor a ship on the
    sea; an edge of the hill kindled with gold,
And the sun rose. Then Clare took home her soul from the
    world and went on. When she was wandering the flats
Of open pasture between the Sur Hill sea-face and the
    great separate sea-dome rock at Point Sur,
Forgetting, as often before, that she and her flock were
    trespassers
In cattle country: she looked and a young cowboy rode
    down from the east. "You'll have to get off this range.
Get out of this field," he said, "your tallow-hoofed mut-
    ton." "Oh," she answered trembling, "I'm going. I
    got lost in the night.
Don't drive them." "A woman?" he said. He jerked the
    reins and sat staring. "Where did *you* drop from?"
    She answered faintly,
With a favor-making smile, "From the south." "Who's with
    you?" "Nobody."
"Keep going, and get behind the hill if you can
Before Nick Miles the foreman looks down this way."
She said to the ram, "Oh Saul, Oh hurry. Come Leader.
Tiny and Frannie and Nosie, we have to go on.
Oh, hurry, Fern." They huddled bleating about her,

[58]

And she in the midst made haste; they pressed against her
And moved in silence. The young cowboy rode on the east
As hoping to hide the flock from Nick Miles his foreman,
Sidelong in the saddle, and gazed at Clare, at the twisting
Ripple of pale bright hair from her brown skin
Behind the temples. She felt that his looks were friendly,
She turned and timidly smiled. Then she could see
That he was not a man but a boy, sixteen
Or seventeen; she felt more courage. "What would your
    foreman
Do if he saw us?" "He'd be rough. But," he said,
"You'll soon be behind the hill. Where are you going?"
She made no answer. "To Monterey?" "Oh...to no-
    where!"
She shivered and sought his face with her eyes. "To no-
    where, I mean."
"Well," he said sulkily, "where did you sleep last night?
Somewhere?" She said with eagerness, "Ah, two miles
    back,
On the edge of the sand; we weren't really in the field."
He stared. "You're a queer one. Is that old coat
All you've got on?" "No, no, there's a dress under it.
But scrubbed so often," she said, "with sand and water
Because I had no soap, it's nothing but rags."
"You needn't hurry, no one can see you now.
... My name's Will Brighton," he said. "Well, mine is
    Clare."
"Where do you live when you're at home, Clare?" "I
    haven't any."
They rounded the second spur of the hill. Gray lupine
    clothed the north flank, a herd of cattle stared down
From the pale slope of dead grass above the gray thicket.
    Rumps high, low quarters, they were part of the
    world's end sag,

The inverted arch from the Sur Hill height to the flat fore-
　　land and up the black lava rock of Point Sur;
In the open gap the mountain sea-wall of the world foam-
　　footed went northward. Beyond the third spur Clare
　　saw
A barn and a house up the wrinkled hill, oak-scrub and
　　sycamores. The house built of squared logs, time-
　　blackened,
Striped with white plaster between the black logs, a tall
　　dead cube with a broken chimney, made her afraid;
Its indestructible crystalline shape. "Oh! There's a house.
They'll see us from there. I'll go back..." "Don't be
　　afraid,"
He answered smiling, "that place has no eyes.
There you can turn your sheep in the old corral,
Or graze them under the buckeyes until evening.
No one will come." She sighed, and then faintly:
"Nobody ever lives there, you're sure?" "Not for eight
　　years.
You can go in," he said nervously: "maybe
You haven't been inside a house a good while?"
She looked up at his pleasant unformed young face,
It was blushing hot. "Oh, what's the matter with the
　　house?"
"Nothing. Our owner bought the ranch, and the house
Stands empty, he didn't want it. They tell me an old man
Claiming to be God... a kind of a preacher boarded there,
And the family busted up." She said "I don't believe
Any such story." "Well, he was kind of a preacher.
They say his girl killed herself; he washed his hands
With fire and vanished." "Then she was crazy. What, spill
Her own one precious life," she said trembling,
"She'd nothing but that? Ah! no!
No matter how miserable, what goes in a moment,

You know ... out ..." Her head bowed, and her hand
Dug anxiously in the deep pads of wool
On the shoulder of the ram walking against her side;
When her face lifted again even the unwatchful boy
Took notice of tears.

They approached the house; the fence
in front was broken but the windows and doors were
whole,
The rose that grew over the rotted porch steps was dead;
yet the sleep of the house seemed incorruptible,
It made Clare and the boy talk low. He dropped out of
the saddle and made the bridle hang down
To serve for tether. "Come round by the back," he whis-
pered, "this door is locked." "What for?" "To go in,"
he whispered.
"Ah no, I have to stay with my sheep. Why in the world
should I go in to your dirty old house?"
His face now he'd dismounted was level with hers; she saw
the straw-colored hairs on his lip, and freckles,
For he'd grown pale. "Hell," he said, narrowing his eyes,
hoping to be manly and bully her: but the heart failed
him,
He said sadly, "I hoped you'd come in." She breathed,
"Oh," her mouth twitching,
But whether with fear or laughter no one could tell,
And said, "You've been kind. Does nobody ever come
here?
Because I'd have to leave my poor friends outdoors,
Some one might come and hurt them." "The sheep?
Oh, nobody
No one can see them. Oh, Clare, come on. Look here,"
He ran and opened a gate, "the corral fence
Is good as new and the grass hasn't been touched."

The small flock entered gladly and found green weeds
In the matted gray. Clare slowly returned. The boy
Catching her by the hand to draw her toward the house,
She saw his young strained face, and wondered. "Have you
    ever
Been, with a woman?" "Ah," he said proudly, "yes."
But the honesty of her gaze dissolving his confidence
He looked at the ground and said mournfully, "She wasn't
    white.
And I think she was quite old . . ." Clare in her turn
Reddened. "If it would make you happy," she said.
"I want to leave glad memories. And you'll not be sorry
After I'm gone?"

                The sheep, missing their mistress,
Bleated and moved uneasily, forgetting to feed,
While Clare walked in the house. She said, "Oh, not yet.
Let's look at the house. What was the man's name
Whose daughter . . . he said he was God and suddenly van-
    ished?"
"A man named Barclay," he said, "kind of a preacher."
They spoke in whispers, peering about. At length Clare
    sighed,
And stripped off the long brown coat.

              When they returned outdoors,
Blinking in the sun, the boy bent his flushed face
Toward Clare's pale one and said, "Dear, you can stay here
As long as you want, but I must go back to work."
She heard the sheep bleating, and said, "Good-by.
Good luck, Will Brighton." She hurried to her flock, while
    he
Mounted, but when he had ridden three strides of a canter

Clare was crying, "Oh help. Oh help. Oo! Oo!"
    He returned,
And found her in the near corner of the corral
On hands and knees, her flock huddling about her,
Peering down a pit in the earth. Oak-scrub and leafless
Buckeyes made a dark screen toward the hill, and Clare
Stood up against it, her white face and light hair
Shining against it, and cried, "Oh, help me, they've fallen,
Two have fallen." The pit was an old well;
The hand-pump had fallen in, and the timbers
That closed the mouth had crumbled to yellow meal.
Clare lay and moaned on the brink among the dark nettles,
Will Brighton brought the braided line that hung
        at his saddle
And made it fast and went down.

                              The well-shaft was so filled up
With earth-fall and stones and rotting timbers, it was pos-
        sible for the boy and girl to hoist up the fallen
Without other contrivance than the looped rope. The one
        came struggling and sobbing, Clare cried her name,
"Oh, Fern, Fern, Fern." She stood and fell, and scrambled
        up to her feet, and plunged on three legs. The other
Came flaccid, it slipped in the rope and hung head down-
        ward, Clare made no cry. When it was laid by the
        well-brink
A slime of half-chewed leaves fell from its mouth. The boy
        climbed up. "While I was making your pleasure,"
Clare said, "this came. While I was lying there. What's
        punished is kindness." He touched the lifeless ewe
        with his foot,
Clare knelt against her and pushed him away. He said, "It
        fell the first and its neck was broken." And Clare:
"This was the one that would nudge my hands

When I was quiet, she'd come behind me and touch me, I
   called her Nosie. One night we were all near frozen
And starved, I felt her friendly touches all night." She
   lifted the head. "Oh, Nosie, I loved you best.
Fern's leg is broken. We'll all be like you in a little while."
   The boy ran and caught Fern, and said
"The bones are all right. A sprain I guess, a bad sprain.
   I'll come in the evening, Clare, if you're still here.
I'm sorry." She sat with the head on her lap, and he rode
   away. After a time she laid it on the earth.
She went and felt Fern's fore-leg and went slowly up the
   hill; her small flock followed.

IV

                              Fern lagged and lagged,
Dibbling the dust with the mere points of the hoof
Of the hurt fore-leg, and rolling up to her shepherdess
The ache of reproachful eyes. "Oh, Fern, Oh, Fern,
What can I do? I'm not a man, to be able to carry you.
My father, he could have carried you." Tears from Clare's
   eyes
Fell in the roadway; she was always either joyful or
   weeping.
They climbed for half the day, only a steep mile
With many rests, and lay on the Sur Hill summit.
The sun and the ocean were far down below, like fire in a
   bowl;
The shadow of the hills lay slanting up a thin mist
Into the eastern sky, dark immense lines
Going out of the world.

                              Clare slept wretchedly, for thirst
And anxious dreams and sorrow. She saw the lighthouse

Glow and flash all night under the hill;
The wind turned south, she smelled the river they had left,
Small flying clouds from the south crossed the weak stars.
In the morning Fern would not walk.

                                  Between noon and morning
A dark-skinned man on a tall hammer-headed
Flea-bitten gray horse rode north on the hill-crest.
Clare ran to meet him. "Please help me. One of my sheep
Has hurt her leg and can't walk. . . . Entiendes inglés?"
She faltered, seeing him Indian-Spanish, and the dark eyes
Gave no sign whether they understood, gazing through her
    with a blue light across them
Like the sea-lions' eyes. He answered easily in English,
    "What can I do?" in the gentle voice of his people;
And Clare: "I thought you might carry her down. We are
    very thirsty, the feed is all dry, here is no water,
And I've been gathering the withered grasses to feed her."
    He said, "We could tie her onto the horse." "Ah, no,
She'd be worse hurt. . . . She's light and little, she was born
    in the hills." The other sheep had followed their shep-
    herdess
Into the road and sadly looked up, the man smiled and dis-
    mounted among them. "Where are you going?"
She answered, "North. Oh, come and see her. Unless you
    carry her
I don't know what we can do." "But it's two miles
Down to the river." The lame ewe, whether frightened
By the stranger and his horse, or rested at length,
Now rose and went quietly to Clare, the hurt fore-leg
Limping but serving. Clare laughed with pleasure. "Oh, now,
We can go down by ourselves. Come Fern, come Saul,
Fay, Frannie, Leader . . ." She was about to have called
The name of the one that died yesterday; her face

Changed and she walked in silence, Fern at her thigh.
The friendly stranger walked on the other side,
And his horse followed the sheep. He said: "I have seen
Many things, of this world and the others, but what are
    you?"
"My name's Clare Walker." "Well, I am Onorio Vasquez.
I meant, what are you doing? I think that I'd have seen
    you or heard of you
If you live near." "I'm doing? I'm taking care of my
    sheep." She looked at his face to be sure of kindness,
And said, "I'm doing like most other people; take care of
    those that need me and go on till I die.
But *I* know when it will be; that's the only ... I'm often
    afraid." Her look went westward to the day moon,
Faint white shot bird in her wane, the wings bent down-
    ward, falling in the clear over the ocean cloud-bank.
"Most people will see hundreds of moons: I shall see five.
When this one's finished." Vasquez looked intently at her
    thin young face, turned sideways from him, the parted
Sun-scarred lips, the high bridge of the nose, dark eyes
    and light hair; she was thin, but no sign of sickness;
    her eyes
Met his and he looked down and said nothing. When he
    looked down he remembered chiefly the smooth brown
    throat
And the little hollow over the notch of the breast-bone. He
    said at length, carefully, "You needn't be afraid.
I often," he murmured shyly, "have visions. I used to
    think they taught me something, but I was a fool.
If you saw a vision, or you heard a voice from heaven, it
    is nothing." She answered, "What I fear really's the
    pain.
The rest is only a kind of strangeness." Her eyes were full
    of tears and he said anxiously, "Oh, never

Let visions nor voices fool you.
They are wonderful but we see them by chance; I think
   they mean something in their own country but they
   mean
Nothing in this; they have nothing to do with our lives and
   deaths." She answered in so changed a voice that Vas-
   quez
Stared; the tears were gone and her eyes were laughing.
   "Oh, no, it was nothing," she said, "in the way of that.
Visions? My trouble is a natural thing.
But tell me about those visions." He muttered to himself
With a shamed face and answered, "Not now." The south
   wind
That drove the dust of the little troop before them
Now increased and struck hard, where the road gained
A look-out point over the fork of the canyon
And the redwood forest below. The sheep were coughing
In the whirl of wind. At this point the lame ewe
Lay down and refused to rise, "Oh, now, now, now,"
Clare wrung her hands, "we're near the water too. We're
   all so thirsty.
Oh, Fern!" Vasquez said sadly, "If she'd be quiet
Over my shoulders, but she won't." He heard a hoarse voice
Cry in the canyon, and Clare softly cried answer
And ran to the brink of the road. She stood there panting
Above the pitch and hollow of the gorge, her grotesque
   cloak
Blown up to her shoulders, flapping like wings
About the half nakedness of the slender body.
Vasquez looked down the way of her gaze, expecting
To see some tragical thing; he saw nothing but a wide heron
Laboring thwart wind from the shore over the heads of the
   redwoods. A heavy dark hawk balanced in the storm
And suddenly darted; the heron, the wings and long legs

wavering in terror, fell, screaming, the long throat
Twisted under the body; Clare screamed in answer. The
    pirate death drove by and had missed, and circled
For a new strike, the poor frightened fisherman
Beat the air over the heads of the redwoods and labored
    upward. Again and again death struck, and the heron
Fell, with the same lost cry, and escaped; but the last fall
Was into the wood, the hawk followed, both passed from
    sight
Under the waving spires of the wood.

                                            Clare Walker
Turned, striving with the gesture of a terrified child
To be quiet, her clenched fist pressed on her mouth,
Her teeth against the knuckles, and her blonde hair
Wild on the wind. "Oh, what can save him, can save him?
Oh, how he cried at each fall!" She crouched in the wind
At the edge of the road, trembling; the ewe called Tiny
Crossed over and touched her, the others turned anxious
    looks
From sniffing the autumn-pinched leaves of the groundling
    blackberries.
When she was quieted Vasquez said, "You love
All creatures alike." She looked at his face inquiringly
With wide candid brown eyes, either not knowing
Or not thinking. He said, "It is now not far
Down to the running water; we'd better stretch her
Across the saddle"— he nodded toward the lame ewe —
"You hold her by the fore-legs and I by the hind ones,
She'll not be hurt." Clare's voice quieted the sheep
And Vasquez' the indignant horse. They came down at
    length
To dark water under gigantic trees.

V

She helped Fern drink before herself drooped eagerly
Her breast against the brown stones and kissed the cold
    stream.
She brought from the bundle what food remained, and
    shared it
With Vasquez and the munching sheep. There were three
    apples
From Fogler's trees, and a little jar of honey
And crumbled comb from his hives, and Clare drew a net
Of water-cress from the autumn-hushed water to freshen
The old bread and the broken biscuits. She was gay with
    delight
At having something to give. They sat on the bank, where
    century
After century of dropping redwood needles had made the
    earth, as if the dark trees were older
Than their own mother.

Clare answered Vasquez' question and said she had
    come from the coast mountains in the south;
She'd left her home a long time ago; and Fogler, the
    farmer by the Big Sur, had given her this food
Because he was sorry his dogs had worried the sheep. But
    yesterday she was passing Point Sur, and Fern
Had fallen into a well by the house. She said nothing of the
    other ewe, that had died; and Vasquez
Seemed to clench himself tight: "What were you doing
    at Point Sur, it's not on the road?" "The sheep were
    hungry,
And I wandered off the road in the dark. It was wicked of
    me to walk in the pasture, but a young cowboy
Helped me on the right way. We looked into the house."

He said, "Let no one go back there, let its mice have it.
God lived there once and tried to make peace with the peo-
    ple; no peace was made." She stared in silence, and
    Vasquez:
"After that time I bawled for death, like a calf for the
    cow. There were no visions. My brothers watched me,
And held me under the hammers of food and sleep."
He ceased; then Clare in a troubled silence
Thought he was lying, for she thought certainly that no one
Ever had desired death. But, for he looked unhappy
And said nothing, she said Will Brighton had told her
Something about a man who claimed to be God,
"Whose daughter," she said, "died." Vasquez stood up
And said trembling, "In the ruin of San Antonio church
I saw an owl as big as one of your sheep
Sleeping above the little gilt Virgin above the altar.
That was no vision. I want to hear nothing
Of what there was at Point Sur." He went to his horse
That stood drooping against the stream-bank, and rode
The steep soft slope between the broad butts of trees.
But, leaving the undisturbed air of the wood
For the rough wind of the roadway, he stopped
        and went back.
"It will rain," he said. "You ought to think of yourself.
The wind is digging water since we came down.
My father's place is too far. There's an old empty cabin
A short ways on." She had been crouching again
Over the stream to drink, and rose with wet lips
But answered nothing. Vasquez felt inwardly dizzy
For no reason he knew, as if a gray bird
Turned in his breast and flirted half open wings
Like a wild pigeon bathing. He said, "You'll see it
Above the creek on the right hand of the road

[70]

Only a little way north." He turned and rode back,
Hearing her call "Good-by," into the wind on the road.

This man was that Onorio Vasquez
Who used to live on Palo Corona mountain
With his father and his six brothers, but now they lived
Up Mill Creek Canyon beside the abandoned lime-kiln
On land that was not their own. For yearly on this coast
Taxes increase, land grows harder to hold,
Poor people must move their places. Onorio had wealth
Of visions, but those are not coinable. A power in his mind
Was more than equal to the life he was born to,
But fear, or narrowing fortune, had kept it shut
From a larger life; the power wasted itself
In making purposeless visions, himself perceived them
To have no meaning relative to any known thing: but al-
    ways
They made him different from his brothers; they gave him
A kind of freedom; they were the jewels and value of his
    life.
So that when once, at a critical time, they failed
And were not seen for a year, he'd hungered to die.
That was nine years ago; his mind was now quieter,
But still it found all its value in visions.
Between them, he hired out his hands to the coast farms,
Or delved the garden at home.

Clare Walker, when he was gone, forgot him at once.
She drank a third draught, then she dropped off her shoes
And washed the dust from her feet. Poor Fern was now
    hobbling
Among the others, and they'd found vines to feed on
At the near edge of the wood, so that Clare felt
Her shepherdess mind at peace, to throw off

The coat and the rags and bathe in the slender stream,
Flattening herself to find the finger's depth water.
The water and the air were cold now, she rubbed her body
Hastily dry with the bleached rags of her dress
And huddled the cloak about her, but hung the other
Over a branch to dry. Sadly she studied
The broken shoes and found them useless at last,
And flung them into the bushes. An hour later
She resumed the dress, she called her flock to go on
Northward. "Come Fern, come Frannie. Oh, Saul.
Leader and Hornie and Tiny, we have to go on."

VI

The sky had blackened and the wind raised a dust
When they came up to the road from the closed quiet of
    the wood,
The sun was behind the hill but not down yet. Clare passed
    the lichen-plated abandoned cabin that Vasquez
Had wished her to use, because there was not a blade of
    pasture about it, nothing but the shafted jealousy
And foodless possession of the great redwoods. She saw
    the gray bed of the Little Sur like a dry bone
Through its winter willows, and on the left in the sudden
Sea-opening V of the canyon the sun streaming through a
    cloud, the lank striped ocean, and an arched film
Of sand blown from a dune at the stream's foot. The road
    ahead went over a bridge and up the bare hill
In lightning zigzags; a small black bead came down the
    lightning, flashing at the turns in the strained light,
A motor-car driven fast, Clare urged her flock into the
    ditch by the road, but the car turned
This side the bridge and glided down a steep driveway.

When Clare came and looked down she saw the farmhouse
Beside the creek, and a hundred bee-hives and a leafless
    orchard,
Crossed by the wheeling swords of the sun.
A man with a gray mustache covering his mouth
Stood by the road, Clare felt him stare at the sheep
And stare at her bare feet, though his eyes were hidden
In the dark of his face in the shadow of the turbid light.
She smiled and murmured, "Good evening." He giggled to
    himself
Like a half-witted person and stared at her feet.
She passed, in the swirls of light and dust, the old man
Followed and called, "Hey: Missy: where will you sleep?"
"Why, somewhere up there," she answered. He giggled,
    "Eh, Eh!
If I were you. Ho," he said joyfully,
"If I were in your *shoes,* I'd look for a roof.
It's big and bare, Serra Hill. You from the south?"
"I've been in the rain before," she answered. She laid
Her hand on a matted fleece. "I've got to find them
Some feeding-place, they're hungry, they've been in the
    hungry
Redwoods." He stopped and peered and giggled:
    "One's lame.
But," he said chuckling, "you could go on all night
And never muddy your shoes. Ho, ho! Listen, Missy.
You ain't a Mexican, I guess you've had bad luck.
I'll fix you up in the hay-shed and you'll sleep dry,
These fellows can feed all night." "The owner," she said,
"Wouldn't let me. They'd spoil the hay." "The owner.
Bless you, the poor old man's too busy to notice.
Paying his debts. That was his sharp son
Drove in just now. They hated the old man
But now they come like turkey-buzzards to watch him die."

"Oh! Is he dying?" "Why, fairly comfortable.
As well as you can expect." "I think, we'll go on,"
She murmured faintly. "Just as you like, Missy.
But nobody cares whether you spoil the hay.
There's plenty more in the barn, and all the stock
'll soon be cleared out. I don't work for his boys.
Ho, it's begun already." Some drops were flying, and the
    sun
Drowned in a cloud, or had set, suddenly the light was
    twilight. The old man waved his hand in the wind
Over the hives and the orchard. "This place," he giggled,
    "meant the world to old Warfield: Hey, watch them
    sell.
It means a shiny new car to each of the boys." He shot up
    the collar of his coat, and the huddling sheep
Tucked in their rumps; the rain on a burst of wind, small
    drops but many. The sheep looked up at their mistress,
Who said, feeling the drift like needles on her cheek, and
    cold drops
Run down by her shoulder, "If nobody minds, you think,
    about our lying in the hay." "Hell no, come in.
Only you'll have to be out in the gray to-morrow, before the
    sharp sons get up." He led her about
By the bridge, through the gapped fence, not to be seen
    from the house.
The hay-shed was well roofed, and walled southward
Against the usual drive of the rain. Clare saw in the
    twilight
Wealth of fodder and litter, and was glad, and the sheep
Entered and fed.

After an hour the old man

Returned, with a smell of fried grease in the gray
    darkness.

[74]

Clare rose to meet him, she thought he was bringing food,
But the odor was but a relic of his own supper.
"It's raining," he said; as if she could fail to hear
The hissing drift on the roof; "you'd be cosy now
On Serra Hill." He paused and seemed deeply thoughtful,
And said, "But still you could walk all night and never
Get your shoes wet. Ho, ho! You're a fine girl,
How do you come to be on the road? Eh? Trouble?"
"I'm going north. You're kind," she said, "people are
      kind."
"Why, yes, I'm a kind man. Well, now, sleep cosy."
He reached into the dark and touched her, she stood
Quietly and felt his hand. A dog was heard barking
Through the hiss of rain. He said, "There's that damn'
      dog.
I tied him up after I let you in,
Now he'll be yelling all night." The old man stumped off
Into the rain, then Clare went back to her sheep
And burrowed in the hay amongst them.

                                    The old man returned
A second time; Clare was asleep and she felt
The sheep lifting their heads to stare at his lantern.
"Oh! What do you want?" "Company, company," he
      muttered.
"They've got an old hatchet-faced nurse in the house. . .
But he's been dying for a month, he makes me nervous.
The boys don't mind, but *I'm* nervous." He kicked
One of the sheep to make it rise and make room,
Clare murmured sadly, "Don't hurt them." He sat
      in the hay
In heavy silence, holding the lantern on knee
As if it were a fretful baby. The fulvous glimmer
Through one of his hands showed the flesh red, and seemed

To etch the bones in it, the gnarled shafts of the fingers
And scaly lumps in the skin. Clare heard the chained dog
     howling,
And the rain had ceased. She reached in pitying tenderness
And touched the old man's illuminated hand and said
"How hard you have worked." "Akh," he groaned, "so
     has he.
And gets . . ." He moved his hand to let the warm light
Lie on her face, so that her face and his own were planets
To the lantern sun; hers smooth except the wind-blistered
     lips, pure-featured, pitying, with large dark eyes
The little sparkles of the reflected lantern had room to
     swim in; his bristly and wrinkled, and the eyes
Like sparks in a bush; the sheep uneasily below the faces
     moved formless, only Saul's watchful head
With the curled horns in the halo of light. The faint and
     farther rays of that sun touched falling spheres
Of water from the eaves at the open side of the shed, or
     lost themselves at the other in cobwebbed corners
And the dust of space. In the darkness beyond all stars the
     little river made a noise. The old man muttered,
"I heard him choking night before last and still he goes on.
It's a hell of a long ways to nothing . . .
You know the best thing to do? Tip this in the straw,"
He tilted the lantern a little, "end in a minute,
In a blaze and yell." She said, "No! no!" and he felt
The hay trembling beside him. The unconscious motion
     of her fear
Was not inward but toward the sheep. He observed
Nothing of that, but giggled to himself to feel
The hay trembling beside him. He dipped his hand
And caught her bare foot; clutching it with his fingers
He scratched the sole with his thumb, but Clare sat quiet
In pale terror of tipping the lantern. The old man

[76]

Groaned and stood up. "You wouldn't sit like a stone
If I were twenty years younger. Oh, damn you," he said,
"You think we get old? I'm the same fresh flame of youth
    still,
Stuck in an old wrinkled filthy rawhide
That soon'll rot and lie choking." She stammered, "Ah,
    no, no,
You oughtn't to think so. You're well and strong. Or maybe
At last it'll come suddenly or while you sleep,
Never a pain." He swung up the lantern
Before his hairy and age-deformed face. "Look at me.
    Pfah!
And still it's April inside." He turned to go out,
Clare whispered, "Oh! Wait." She stood wringing her
    hands,
Warm light and darkness in waves flushing and veiling
Her perplexed face, the lantern in the old man's fist
Swinging beyond his body. "Oh, how can I tell?"
She said trembling. "You see: I'll never come back:
If anything I could do would give you some pleasure;
And you wouldn't be sorry after I'm gone." He turned,
Stamping his feet. "Heh?" He held up the lantern
And stared at her face and giggled. She heard the sheep
Nestling behind her and saw the old man's mouth
Open to speak, a black hole under the grizzled thatch,
And close again on round silence. "I'd like to make you
Happier," she faltered. "Heh?" He seemed to be trembling
Even more than Clare had trembled; he said at length,
"Was you in earnest?" "I had a great trouble,
So that now nothing seems hard . . .
That a shell broke and truly I love all people.
I'll . . . it's a little thing . . . my time is short."
He stood giggling and fidgeting. "Heh, heh! You be good.
I've got to get my sleep. I was just making the rounds.

He makes me nervous, that old man. It's his stomach
Won't hold nothing. You wouldn't play tricks to-night
And the old man puking his last? Now, you lie down.
Sleep cosy," he said. The lantern went slowly winking
        away,
And she was left among the warm sheep, and thoughts
Of death, and to hear the stream; and again the wind
Raved in the dark.

              She dreamed that a two-legged whiff of flame
Rose up from the house gable-peak crying, "Oh! Oh!"
And doubled in the middle and fled away on the wind
Like music above the bee-hives.

                    At dawn a fresh burst of rain
Delayed her, and two of the sheep were coughing. She
        thought that no unfriendly person would come in the
        rain,
And hoped the old man might think to bring her some food,
        she was very hungry. The house-dog that all night long
Had yapped his chain's length, suddenly ran into the shed,
        then Clare leaped up in fear for the sheep, but this
Was a friendly dog, loving to fondle and be fondled, he
        shook his sides like a mill-wheel and remained amongst
        them.
The rain paused and returned, the sheep fed so contentedly
Clare let them rest all morning in the happy shelter, she
        dulled her own hunger with sleep. About noon
She lifted her long staff from the hay and stood up. "Come
        Saul, come little Hornie,
Fay, Fern and Frannie and Leader, we have to go on.
Tiny, Tiny, get up. Butt and Ben, come on":
These were the two old wethers: and she bade the dog
"Good-by, good-by." He followed however; but at length

[*78*]

Turned back from the crooked road up the open hill
When cold rain fell. Clare was glad of that, yet she wished
She'd had something to give him.

VII

 She gained the blasty hill-top,
The unhappy sheep huddling against her thighs,
And so went northward barefoot in the gray rain,
Abstractedly, like a sleepwalker on the ridge
Of his inner necessity, or like
Some random immortal wish of the solitary hills.
If you had seen her you'd have thought that she always
Walked north in the rain on the ridge with the sheep about
 her.
Yet sometimes in the need of a little pleasure
To star the gray, she'd stop in the road and kiss
One of the wet foreheads: but then run quickly
A few steps on, as if loitering were dangerous,
You'd have pitied her to see her.

 Over Mescal Creek
High on the hill, a brook in a rocky gulch, with no canyon,
Light-headed hunger and cold and the loneliness unlocked
Her troubled mind, she talked and sang as she went. "I
 can't eat the cold cress, but if there were acorns,
Bitter acorns. Ai chinita que si,
Ai que tu dami tu amor. Why did you
Have to go dry at the pinch, Frannie? Poor thing, no mat-
 ter. Que venga con migo chinita
A donde vivo yo.
I gave them all my bread, the poor shipwrecked people,
 and they wanted more." She trembled and said,
 "They're cruel,

But they were hungry. They'll never catch us I think.
Oh, hurry, hurry." With songs learned from the shepherd
    she came to the fall of the road into Mill Creek
    Canyon.
Two of the sheep were sick and coughing, and Clare
    looked down. Flying bodies of fog, and unending fleet
Of formless gray ships in a file fled down the great canyon
Tearing their keels over the redwoods; Clare watched them
    and sang, "Oh, golondrina, oh, darting swallow,"
And heard the ocean like the blood in her ears. The west-
    covered sun stared a wan light up-canyon
Against the cataract of little clouds.

                         The two coughing sheep
Brought her to a stand; then she opened their mouths
    and found
Their throats full of barbed seeds from the bad hay
Greedily eaten; and the gums about their teeth
Were quilled with the wicked spikes; which drawn,
    thin blood
Dripped from the jaw. The folds of the throat her fingers
Could not reach nor relieve; thereafter, when they coughed,
Clare shook with pain. Her pity poisoned her strength.

                        Unhappy shepherdess,
Numbed feet and hands and the face
Turbid with fever:
You love, and that is no unhappy fate,
Not one person but all, does it warm your winter?
Walking with numbed and cut feet
Along the last ridge of migration
On the last coast above the not-to-be-colonized
Ocean, across the streams of the people
Drawing a faint pilgrimage

As if you were drawing a line at the end of the world
Under the columns of ancestral figures:
So many generations in Asia,
So many in Europe, so many in America:
To sum the whole. Poor Clare Walker, she already
Imagines what sum she will cast in April.

                                    She came by the farmhouse
At Mill Creek, then she wavered in the road and went to
      the door,
Leaving her sheep in the road; the day was draining
Toward twilight. Clare began to go around the house,
Then stopped and returned and knocked faintly at the door.
No answer; but when she was turning back to the road
The door was opened, by a pale slight young man
With no more chin than a bird, and Mongol-slanted
Eyes; he peered out, saying, "What do you want?" Clare
      stood
Wringing the rain from her fingers. "Oh, oh," she stam-
      mered,
"I don't know what. I have some sheep with me.
I don't know where we can stay." He stood in the door
And looked afraid. The sheep came stringing down
Through the gate Clare had left open. A gray-eyed man
With a white beard pushed by the boy and said
"What does she want? What, are you hungry? Take out
      your beasts,
We can't have sheep in the yard." Clare ran to the gate,
"Come Leader, come Saul." The old man returned indoors,
Saying, "Wait outside, I'll get you some bread." Clare
      waited,
Leaning against the gate, it seemed a long while;
The old man came back with changed eyes and changed
      voice:

"We can't do anything for you. There isn't any bread.
Move on from here." She said through her chattering
    teeth,
"Come Saul, come Leader, come Frannie. We have to go on.
Poor Fern, come on." They drifted across the Mill Creek
    bridge
And up the road in the twilight. "The ground-squirrels,"
    she said, "hide in their holes
All winter long, and the birds have perches but we have no
    place." They tried to huddle in the heart of a bush
Under a redwood, Clare crouched with the sheep about her,
    her thighs against her belly, her face on her knees,
Not sleeping, but in a twilight consciousness, while the
    night darkened. In an hour she thought she must move
    or die.
"Ah little Hornie," she said, feeling with shrivelled fingers
    the sprouts of the horns in the small arched forehead,
"Come Fern: are you there, Leader? Come Saul, come
    Nosie . . . Ah, no, I was dreaming. Oh, dear," she whis-
    pered, "we're very
Miserable now." She crept out of the bush and the sheep
    followed; she couldn't count them, she heard them
Plunge in the bush and heard them coughing behind her.
    They came on the road
In the gray dark; there, though she'd meant to go north
She went back toward the farmhouse. Crossing the bridge
She smelled oak-smoke and thought of warmth. Grown
    reckless
Clare entered the farmhouse yard with her fleeced follow-
    ing,
But not daring enough to summon the door
Peered in a window. What she saw within
Mixed with her fever seemed fantastic and dreadful. It was
    nothing strange:

[*82*]

The weak-faced youth, the bearded old man, and two old
women
Idle around a lamp on a table. They sat on their chairs
in the warmth and streaming light and nothing
Moved their faces. But Clare felt dizzy at heart, she
thought they were waiting for death: how could they
sit
And not run and not cry? Perhaps they were dead al-
ready? Then, the old man's head
Turned, and the youth's fingers drummed on his chair.
One of the blank old women was sewing and the other
Frowned and breathed. She lifted and spoke to whitebeard,
then the first old woman
Flashed eyes like rusty knives and sheathed them again
And sewed the cloth; they grew terribly quiet;
Only the white beard quivered. The young man stood up
And moved his mouth for a good while but no one
Of those in the room regarded him. He sighed and saw
Clare's face at the window. She leaped backward; the
lamplight
Had fed her eyes with blindness toward the gray night,
She ran in a panic about the barren garden,
Unable to find the gate; the sheep catching her fear
Huddled and plunged, pricking the empty wet earth with
numberless hoof-prints. But no one came out pursuing
them,
The doors were not opened, the house was quiet. Clare
found the gate
And stood by it, whispering, "Dear Tiny. Ah, Fern, that's
you. Come Saul," she fumbled each head as it passed
the gate-post,
To count the flock.
                    But all had not passed, a man on a horse
Came plodding the puddled road. Clare thought the world

Was all friendly except in that house, and she ran
To the road's crown. "Oh, Oh," she called; and Onorio
Vasquez answered, "I rode early in the morning
To find you and couldn't find you. I've been north and
     south.
I thought I could find the track of the sheep." She an-
     swered
Through chattering teeth, "I thought I could stand the rain.
I'm sick and the sheep are sick." He said gravely
"There's hardly a man on the coast wouldn't have helped
     you
Except in that house. There, I think they *need* help.
Well, come and we'll live the night." "How far?" she sighed
Faintly, and he said "Our place is away up-canyon,
You'll find it stiff traveling by daylight even.
To-night's a camp."

                    He led her to the bridge, and there
Found dry sticks up the bank, leavings of an old flood,
     under the spring of the timbers,
And made a fire against the creekside under the road for
     a roof. He stripped her of the dripping cloak
And clothed her in his, the oil-skin had kept it dry, and
     spread her the blanket from under his saddle to lie on.
The bridge with the tarred road-bed on it was a roof
Over their heads; the sheep, when Clare commanded them,
   lay down like dogs by the fire. The horse was tethered
To a clump of willow in the night outside.

                         When her feet
     and her hands began to be warm he offered her food,
She ate three ravenous mouthfuls and ran from the fire
     and vomited. He heard her gasping in the night thicket
And a new rain. He went after while and dragged her
Back to the frugal fire and shelter of the bridge.

VIII

She lay and looked up at the great black timbers, the
    flapping fire-shadows,
And draggled cobwebs heavy with dirt and water;
While Vasquez watched the artery in the lit edge
Of her lean throat jiggle with its jet of blood
Like a slack harp-string plucked: a toneless trembling:
It made him grieve.

        After a time she exclaimed
"My sheep. My sheep. Count them." "What," he said, "they
    all
Are here beside you." "I never dreamed," she answered,
"That any were lost, Oh no! But my sight swam
When I looked at them in the bad light." He looked
And said "Are there not ... ten?" "No, nine," she an-
    swered.
"Nosie has died. Count them and tell me the truth."
He stood, bowing down his head under the timbers,
And counted seven, then hastily the first two
A second time, and said "Nine." "I'm glad of that,"
She sighed, and was quiet, but her quill fingers working
The border of the saddle blanket. He hoped she would soon
Sleep.

     The horse tethered outside the firelight
Snorted, and the sheep lifted their heads, a spot of white
Came down the dark slope. Vasquez laid his brown palm
Over Clare's wrists, "Lie still and rest. The old fellow
    from the house is coming.
Sleep if you can, I'll talk to him." "Is there a dog?" she
    whispered trembling. "No, no, the old man is alone."
Who peered under the heavy stringer of the bridge, his

beard shone in the firelight. "Here," he shouted, "Hey!
Burn the road, would you? You want to make people stay
    home
And suck the sour bones in their own houses? Come out of
    that hole." But Vasquez: "Now, easy, old neighbor.
    She wanted
Fire and a roof, she's found what you wouldn't give." "By
    God, and a man to sleep with," he said, "that's lucky,
But the bridge, the bridge." "Don't trouble, I'm watching
    the fire. Fire's tame, this weather." The old man stood
    twitching and peering,
And heard the sheep coughing in their cave
Under the road. He squinted toward Clare, and muttered
    at length meekly, "Let me stay a few minutes.
To sit by the little road-fire of freedom. My wife and my
    sister have hated each other for thirty years,
And I between them. It makes the air of the house. I some-
    times think I can see it boil up like smoke
When I look back at the house from the hill above."
    Vasquez said gravely
"I have often watched that." He answered "You haven't
    lived in it. They sit in the house and feed on their own
    poison
And live forever. I am now too feeble with age to escape."
    Clare Walker lifted her head, and faintly:
"Oh stay," she said, "I wish I could gather all that are
    unhappy
Before I die. But why do they hate each other?"
"Their nature," he answered, "old women." She sighed
    and lay down.
"I shan't grow old." "Young fellow," the old man said
    wearily
To Vasquez, "they all make that promise, they never
    keep it.

Life glides by and the bright loving creatures
Eat us in the evening. I'd have given this girl bread
And meat, but my hawks were watching me." He'd found
    a stone
On the edge of the creek, the other side of the fire, and
    squatted there, his two fists
Closing his eyes, the beard shimmering between the bent
    wrists. His voice being silent they heard the fire
Burst the tough bark of a wet branch; the wind turned
    north, then a gust of hail spattered in the willows
And checked at once, the air became suddenly cold. The
    old man lifted his face: "Ah can't you talk?
I thought you'd be gay or I'd not have stayed here, you
    too've grown old? I wish that a Power went through
    the world
And killed people at thirty when the ashes crust them. You,
    cowboy, die, your joints will begin to crackle,
You've had the best. Young bank-clerk, you've had the
    best, grow fat and sorry and more dollars? Here,
    farmer, die,
You've spent the money: will you bleed the mortgage
Fifty years more? You, cunning pussy of the world, you've
    had the fun and the kissing, skip the diseases.
Oh you, you're an honest wife and you've made a baby:
    why should you watch him
Grow up and spoil, and dull like cut lead? I see, my dear,
    you'll never be filled till you grow poisonous,
With eyes like rusty knives under the gray eyebrows. God
    bless you, die." He had risen from the stone, and
    trampled,
Each condemnation, some rosy coal fallen out at the fire's
    edge
Under his foot as if it had been a life. "Sharp at thirty,"
    he said. Clare vaguely moaned

And turned her face to the outer darkness, then Vasquez,
Misunderstanding her pain, thinking it stemmed
From the old man's folly: "Don't mind him, he's not in
  earnest.
These nothing-wishers of life are never in earnest;
Make mouths to scare you: if they meant it they'd do it
And not be alive to make mouths." She made no answer,
But lay and listened to her own rustling pulse-beat,
Her knees drawn up to her breast. White-beard knelt down
  and mended the fire,
And brushed his knees. "There's another law that I'd
  make: to burn the houses. Turn out the people on the
  roads,
And neither homes nor old women we'd be well off. All
  young, all gay, all moving, free larks and foolery
By gipsy fires." His voice fell sad: "It's bitter to be a
  reformer: with two commandments
I'd polish the world a-shining, make the sun ashamed."
Clare Walker stood up, then suddenly sought the dark
  night
To hide herself in the bushes; her bowels were loosened
With cold and fever. Vasquez half rose to follow her,
And he understood, and stayed by the fire. Then white-
  beard
Winking and nodding whispered: "Is she a good piece?
Hey, is she sick? I have to protect my son.
Where in hell did she get the sheep?" Vasquez said fiercely,
"You'd better get home, your wife'll be watching for you.
This girl is sick and half starved, I was unwilling
To let her die in the road." The old man stood up
As pricked with a pin at the thought of home. "What?
  We're free men,"
He said, lifting his feet in an anxious dance
About the low fire: "but it's devilish hard

To be the earthly jewel of two jealous women."
"Look," Vasquez said, "it seems to me that your house is
    afire.
I see rolls of tall smoke..." "By God," he answered,
"I wish it were," he trotted up to the road
While a new drift of hail hissed in the willows,
Softening to rain.

When he was gone, Vasquez
Repaired the fire, and called "Clare! Come in to shelter.
Clare, come! The rain is dangerous for you. The old fool's
    gone home."
He stumbled in the dark along the strand of the creek,
Calling "Clare, Clare!" then looking backward he saw
The huddle of firelit fleeces moving and rising,
And said "The sheep are scattering away to find you.
You ought to call them." She came then, and stood by
    the fire.
He heard the bleating cease, and looked back to see her
Quieting her friends, wringing the rain from her hair,
The fire had leaped up to a blaze. Vasquez returned
Under the bridge, then Clare with her lips flushed
And eyes brilliant with fever: "That poor old man, has he
    gone?
I'm sorry if he's gone.
My father was old, but after he'd plowed the hill-top I've
    seen him ride
The furrows at a dead run, sowing the grain with both
    hands, while he controlled the colt with his knees.
The time it fell at the furrow's end
In the fat clay, he was up first and laughing. He was kind
    and cruel." "Your father?" he said. She answered
"I can't remember my mother, she died to bear me, as I...
    We kept her picture, she looked like me,

And often my father said I was like her.— Oh what's be-
come of the poor old man, has he gone home?
Here he was happy." "Yes, had to go home," he answered.
"But you must sleep. I'll leave you alone if you like,
You promise to stay by the fire and sleep." "Oh I couldn't,
truly. My mind's throwing all its wrecks on the shore
And I can't sleep. That was a shipwreck that drove us
wandering. I remember all things. Your name's Onorio
Vasquez: I wish you had been my brother." He smiled and
touched her cold hand. "For then," she said, "we
could talk
Old troubles asleep: I haven't thought, thought,
For a long while, to-night I can't stop my thoughts. But
we all must die?" "Spread out your hands to the fire,
Warm yourself, Clare." "No, no," she answered, her teeth
chattering, "I'm hot.
My throat aches, yet you see I don't cough, it was Frannie
coughing.— It was almost as if I killed my father,
To swear to the lies I told after he was killed, all to save
Charlie. Do you think he'd care, after . . .
He was surely dead? You don't believe we have spirits?
Nobody believes we have spirits." He began to answer,
And changed his words for caution. "Clare: all you are
saying
Is hidden from me. It's like the visions I have,
That go from unknown to unknown." He said proudly,
"I've watched, the whole night of a full moon, an army of
centaurs
Come out of the ocean, plunging on Sovranes reef
In wide splendors of silver water,
And swim with their broad hooves between the reef and
the shore and go up
Over the mountain — I never knew why.

What you are saying is like that." "Oh, I'll tell you . . ."
   "To-morrow,"
He pleaded, remembering she'd eaten nothing and seeing
The pulse like a plucked harp-string jiggle in her throat;
He felt like a pain of his own the frail reserves of
   her body
Burn unreplenished. "Oh, but I'll tell you: so then
You'll know me, as if we'd been born in the same house,
You'll tell me not to be afraid: maybe I'll sleep
At the turn of night. Onorio — that's really your name?
How stately a name you have — lie down beside me.
I am now so changed: every one's lovely in my eyes
Whether he's brown or white or that poor old man:
In those days nobody but Charlie Maurice
Seemed very dear, as if I'd been blind to all the others.
He lived on the next hill, two miles across a deep valley,
   and then it was five to the next neighbor
At Vicente Springs; people are so few there. We lived a
   long way south, where the hills fall straight to the sea,
And higher than these. He lived with his people. We used
   to meet near a madrone-tree, Charlie would kiss me
And put his hands on my breasts under my clothes. It was
   quite long before we learned the sweet way
That brings much joy to most living creatures, but brought
   us misery at last.

IX

            "My father," she said,
"Had lived there for thirty years, but after he sold his
   cattle
And pastured sheep, to make more money, the neighbors
Were never our friends. Oh, they all feared my father;
Sometimes they threatened our shepherd, a Spanish man

Who looked like you, but was always laughing. He'd laugh
And say 'Guarda a Walker!' so then they'd leave him.
But we lived lonely.

One morning of great white clouds
gliding from the sea,
When I was with Charlie in the hollow near the madrones,
I felt a pleasure like a sweet fire: for all
My joy before had been in *his* pleasure: but this was my
own, it frightened me." She stopped speaking, for
Vasquez
Stood up and left her: he went and sat by the fire. Then
Clare:
"Why do you leave me, Onorio? Are you angry now?"
"I am afraid," he answered, "of this love.
My visions are the life of my life: if I let the pitcher
Break on the rock and the sun kill the stars,
Life would be emptier than death." Her mind went its
own way,
Not understanding so strange a fear: "The clouds were as
bright as stars and I could feel them," she said,
"Through the shut lids of my eyes while the sweet fire
Poured through my body: I knew that some dreadful pain
would pay for such joy. I never slept after that
But dreamed of a laughing child and wakened with running
tears. After I had trembled for days and nights
I asked Tia Livia — that was our shepherd's cousin, she
helped me keep house — what sign tells women
When they have conceived: she told me the moon then
ceases
To rule our blood. I counted the days then,
Not dreaming that Tia Livia would spy and talk.
Was that not strange? I think that she told the shepherd
too,

[92]

And the shepherd had warned my lover: for Charlie failed
Our meeting time, but my father was there with a gray
    face.
In silence, he didn't accuse me, we went home together.

"I met my lover in another place. 'Oh Charlie,
Why do you wear a revolver?' He said the mountain
Was full of rattlers, 'We've killed twenty in a week.
There never have been so many, step carefully sweetheart.'
Sweetheart he called me: you're listening, Onorio?
'Step carefully by the loose stones.' We were too fright-
    ened that day
To play together the lovely way we had learned.

"The next time that I saw him, he and my father
Met on a bare hill-top against a gray cloud.
I saw him turn back, but then I saw that he was ashamed
To seem afraid of a man on the ridge of earth,
With the hills and the ocean under his feet: and my father
    called him.— What was that moan?" She stopped, and
    Vasquez
Heard it far off, and heard the sap of a stick whistle in
    the fire. "Nothing," he said, "low thunder
Far out the ocean, or the surf in the creek-mouth." "— I
    was running up the steep slope to reach them, the
    breath in my heart
Like saw-grass cut me, I had no power to cry out, the
    stones and the broken stubble flaked under my feet
So that I seemed running in one place, unable to go up. It
    was not because he hated my father,
But he was so frightened. They stood as if they were
    talking, a noise of smoke
Blew from between them, my father turned then and
    walked

[*93*]

Slowly along the cloud and sat on the hill-top
As if he were tired.
I said after a time, without thinking,
'Go home, Charlie. I'll say that he killed himself.
And give me the revolver, I'll say it was his.'
So Charlie did.
But when the men came up from Salinas I told my lie
So badly that they believed I was the murderer.
I smelled the jail a long while. I saw the day moon
Down the long street the morning I was taken to court,
As weary-looking and stained as if it were something
    of mine.
I remembered then, that since I came there my blood
Had never been moved when the moon filled: what Livia'd
    told me.
So then I told them my father took his own life
Because the sheep had a sickness and I was pregnant.
The shepherd and Livia swore that they saw him do it.
I'd have been let home:
But the fever I'd caught gathered to a bursting pain,
I had to be carried from the courthouse to the hospital
And for a time knew nothing.
When I began to see with my eyes again
The doctor said: 'The influenza that takes
Many lives has saved yours, you'll not have a child.
Listen,' he said, 'my girl, if you're wise.
Your miscarriage is your luck. Your pelvis — the bones
    down there
Are so deformed that it's not possible for you
To bear a living baby: no life can pass there:
And yours would be lost. You'd better remember,
And try not to be reckless.' I remember so well, Onorio.
I have good reason to remember. You never could guess
What a good reason.

My little king was dead
And I was too weak to care. I have a new king.

"When I got home," she said patiently,
"Everybody believed that I was a murderer;
And Charlie was gone. They left me so much alone
That often I myself believed it. I'd lead the sheep to
    that hill,
There were fifty left out of three hundred,
And pray for pardon."

                            Sleep and her fever confused her
    brain,
One heard phrases in the running babble, across a new
    burst of hail. "Forgive me, father, for I didn't
Know what I was doing." And, "Why have you forsaken
    me, father?" Her mind was living again the bare
    south hill-top
And the bitter penitence among the sheep. "The two men
    that I loved and the baby that I never saw,
All taken away."

                        Then Vasquez was calling her name to
    break the black memories; she turned on her side, the
    flame-light
Leaped, and he saw her face puckering with puzzled won-
    der. "Not all alone? But how can that be?"
She sighed and said, "Oh Leader, don't stray for a while.
    Dear Saul: can you keep them here on the hill around
    me
Without my watching? No one else helps me. I'll lie down
    here on the little grass in the windy sun
And think whether I can live. I have *you,* dear stragglers.

Thoughts come and go back as lightly as deer on the
        hill,
But as hard to catch. . . . Not *all* alone. Oh.
        Not alone at *all*.
Indeed it is even stranger than I thought."

                                                    She laughed
        and sat up. "Oh sweet warm sun . . .
Are you there, Onorio? But where's the poor old man
Who seemed to be so unhappy? I wish he hadn't gone
        home,
For now I remember what I ought to tell him. I'm sadly
        changed
Since that trouble and sickness, and though I'm happy
I hardly ever remember in the nick o' time
What ought to be said. You must tell him
That all our pain comes from restraint of love."
The hail had suddenly hushed, and all her words
Were clear but hurried. "I learned it easily, Onorio,
And never have thought about it again till now. The only
        wonder's
Not to've known always. The beetle beside my hand in the
        grass and the little brown bird tilted on a stone,
The short sad grass, burnt on the gable of the world with
        near sun and all winds: there was nothing there that
        I didn't
Love with my heart, yes the hill though drunk with dear
        blood: I looked far over the valley at the patch
        of oaks
At the head of a field, where Charlie's people had lived
        (they had moved away) and loved them, although
        they'd been
Always unfriendly I never thought of it." Then Vasquez,
        for the first time forgetting the person a moment

[*96*]

To regard the idea: "You were cut off from the natural
    objects of love, you turned toward others." "Ah," she
    answered
Eagerly, "I'd always been turned to all others,
And tired my poor strength confining the joy to few. But
    now I'd no more reason to confine it, I'd nothing
Left to lose nor keep back.— Has the poor old man gone?
He seemed to be truly unhappy.
Wasn't he afraid we'd burn the bridge: we ought surely
To have drowned our fire. I was sick, or I'd have done . . .
    anything.
But old men are so strange, to want and not want,
And then be angry."

                "He has gone," he answered.
"Now, Clare, if you could eat something, then sleep,
To fill the cup for to-morrow."
"I have to tell you the rest.— Why did he go?
Was he angry at me?— Oh, I feel better, Onorio,
But never more open-eyed.

                There was one of those great
    owly hawks
That soar for hours, turning and turning below me along
    the bottom of the slope: I so loved it
I thought if it were hungry I'd give it my hand for meat.

                    Then winter came.
Then about Christmas time (because I'd counted the
    months and remembered Christmas) storm followed
    storm
Like frightened horses tethered to a tree, around and
    around. Three men came in the door without knock-
    ing,

Wherever they moved, water and black oil ran down.
There'd been a shipwreck. I gave them the house,
then one of them
Found the axe and began chopping firewood, another went
back across wild rain to the fall of the hill
And shouted. He was so big, like a barrel walking, I ran
in his shelter
And saw the great, black, masted thing almost on shore,
lying on its side in the shadow of the hill,
And the flying steam of a fire they'd built on the beach.
All that morning the people came up like ants,
Poor souls they were all so tired and cold, some hurt and
some crying. I'd only," she said, "a few handfuls of
flour
Left in the house." She trembled and lay down. "I can't
remember any more."

                        Vasquez made up the fire,
And went and drew up the blanket over Clare's shoulder.
He found her shuddering. "Now sleep. Now rest." She
answered:
"They killed a sheep. They were hungry.
I'd grown to love so much the flock that was left.
Our shepherd, I think, had taken them away mostly
While I was kept in Salinas.
I heard her crying when they threw her down, she thought
I could save her.
Her soft white throat.

"That night I crept out in the thin rain at moonrise
And led them so far away, all that were left,
The house and the barn might hold a hundred hungry
mouths
To hunt us all night and day and could never find us.

[*98*]

We hid in oak-woods. There was nothing to eat,
And never any dry place. We walked in the gray rain in
    the flowing gorges of canyons that no one
But the hawks have seen, and climbed wet stone and saw
    the storms racing below us, but still the thin rain
Sifted through the air as if it fell from the stars. I was
    then much stronger
Than ever since then.

                        A man caught me at last, when I was
    too weak to run, and conquered my fear.
He was kind, he promised me not to hurt the poor flock,
But the half of them had been lost, I never could remember
    how. He lived alone; I was sick in his cabin
For many days, dreaming that a monkey nursed me: he
    looked so funny, he'd a frill of red hair
All around his face.

                        When I grew better, he wanted to do
    like Charlie. I knew what the doctor had said,
But I was ashamed to speak of death: I was often ashamed
    in those days: he'd been so kind. Yet terror
Would come and cover my head like a cold wave.
I watched the moon, but at the full moon my fear
Flowed quietly away in the night.

"The spring and summer were full of pleasure and
    happiness.
I'd no more fear of my friend, but we met seldom. I went
    in freedom
From mountain to mountain, wherever good pasture grew,
Watching the creeks grow quiet and color themselves
With cool green moss, and the green hills turn white.
The people at the few farms all knew me, and now

Their minds changed; they were kind. All the deer
    knew me;
They'd walk in my flock.

                  In the midst of summer,
When the moon filled, my blood failed to be moved,
The life that will make death began in my body.
I'd seen that moon when it was little as a chip
Over my left shoulder, from Palos ridge
By a purple cloud.

X

            "Oh, not till April," she said.
"All's quiet now, the bitterness is past, I have made peace
With death except in my dreams, those can't be ruled. But
    then, when I first
Began to believe and knew it had happened ... I felt
    badly. I went back to my father's house,
Much was broken and chopped down, but I found
Little things that I'd loved when I was a child, hidden in
    corners. When I was drunk with crying
We hurried away. The lambs never seemed able to live, the
    mothers were glad to give me their milk,
We hid in the secret hills till it seemed desolate to die
    there.— Tell me, Onorio,
What month is this?"

                  He answered, "Clare, Clare, fear
    nothing.
Death is as far away from you as from any one.
There was a girl (I've heard my brothers talking:
The road-overseer's daughter) was four or five months
    along

[*100*]

And went to a doctor: she had no trouble:
She's like a virgin again." Clare struck the earth with her
     hands
And raised her body, she stared through the red of the fire
With brilliant confused eyes. "Your face was like a devil's
     in the steamy glimmer:
But only because you don't understand. Why, Tia Livia
     herself . . .you are too innocent, Onorio,
Has done so . . . but women often have small round stones
Instead of hearts." "But," he answered, "if you're not
     able to bear it. Not even a priest would bid you die
For a child that couldn't be born alive. You've lived too
     much alone, bodiless fears have become
Giants in secret. I too am not able to think clearly to-
     night, in the stinging drift of the fire
And the strange place, to-morrow I'll tell you plainly.
     My mind is confused
As I have sometimes felt it before the clouds of the world
Were opened: but I know: for disease to refuse cure
Is self-murder, not virtue." She squatted upright,
Wrapping the coat about her shoulders and knees,
And said, "Have you never seen in your visions
The golden country that our souls came from,
Before we looked at the moon and stars and knew
They are not perfect? We came from a purer peace
In a more perfect heaven; where there was nothing
But calm delight, no cold, no sickness, no sharp hail,
The haven of neither hunger nor sorrow,
But all-enfolding love and unchangeable joy
Near the heart of life." Vasquez turned from the fire
And stared at her lit face. "How did you learn
This wonder? It is true." "I remembered it,"
She answered, "when I was in trouble." "This is the bitter-
     sweet memory,"

He said, "that makes the breast of the earth bitter

After we are born and the dear sun ridiculous. We shall
return there, we homesick."

"No," she answered. "The place was my mother's body
before I was born. You may remember it a little but
I've

Remembered plainly: and the wailing pain of entering this
air. I've thought and thought and remembered. I
found

A cave in a high cliff of white stone, when I was hiding
from people: it was there I had the first memory.

There I'd have stayed in the safe darkness forever; the
sheep were hungry and strayed out, so I couldn't stay.

I remembered again when I went home to our house and
the door hung crazy

On a snapped hinge. You don't believe me, Onorio,

But after while you'll remember plainly, if some long
trouble

Makes you want peace; or being handled has broken your
shame. I have no shame now." He answered nothing
Because she seemed to speak from a frantic mind.

After a moment, "No matter," she said. "When I was in
my worst trouble

I knew that the child was feeding on peace and happiness.
I had happiness here in my body. It is not mine,

But I am its world and the sky around it, its loving God.
It is having the prime and perfect of life,

The nine months that are better than the ninety years. I'd
not steal one of its days to save my life.

I am like its God, how could I betray it? It has not moved
yet

But feels its blessedness in its quietness; but soon I shall
feel it move, Tia Livia said it will nestle

Down the warm nest and flutter like a winged creature. It
    shook her body, she said." But Vasquez, loathing
To hear these things, labored with the sick fire
In the steam of the wet wood, not listening, then Clare
Sighed and lay down. He heard her in a moment
Miserably sobbing, he went and touched her. "What is it?
Clare? Clare?" "Ai, when will morning come?
It is horrible to lie still," she said, "feeling
The black of April . . . it's nothing, it's nothing . . .
    like a cat
Tick tick on padded feet. Ah let me alone, will you?
Lying quiet does it: I'll have courage in my time."

A little later she asked for food, she ate,
And drank from the stream, and slept. She moved
    in her sleep
And tossed her arms, Vasquez would cover them again,
But the fever seemed quieted. He crossed the stream by
    the stones in the dull fire-glimmer
And fetched armfuls of flood-wood from under the oppo-
    site bridge-head. The fire revived; the earth turned
    past midnight;
Far eastward beyond the coasts of the continent morning
    troubled the Atlantic.

XI

                    Vasquez crouched by the fire
And felt one of those revelations that were in his own
    regard the jewels and value of his life
Approach and begin. First passed — as always
Since Barclay was gone, whom he had taken for incarnate
    God — ancestral forms against the white cloud,

[*103*]

The high dark heads of Indian migrations, going south
    along the coast, drawn down from the hungry straits
    and from Asia,
The heads like worn coins and the high shoulders,
The brown-lipped patient mouths below vulture beaks, and
    burnished fall of black hair over slant foreheads,
Going up to the Mayan and the Aztec mountains, and
    sowing the coast. They swept the way and the cloud
    cleared,
The vision would come: came instead a strong pause.

A part
    of his mind
Wished to remember what the rest had forgotten,
And groping for it in the dark withstood the prepared
Pageant of dreams. He'd read in his curious boyhood
Of the child the mother is found incapable of bearing
Cut from the mother's belly. Both live: the wound
Heals: it was called the Cæsarean section. But he, fearing
Whatever thought might threaten to infringe his careful
Chastity of mind, had quickly canceled the memory;
That now sought a new birth; it might save Clare
If he could think of it.

That revived part
Made itself into the vision, all to no purpose,
His precious dreams were never to the point of life.
Only the imperial name and the world's
Two-thousand-year and ten-thousand-miles-traveled
Cæsarean memory appeared. He imagined at first that
    the voice
Cried "Ave Maria," but it cried "Ave Cæsar."

He saw the
    firelight-gilded

[*104*]

Timbers of the bridge above; and one of the ewes lifted
    her head in the light beside Clare sleeping;
The smoke gathered its cloud into a floating globe and
    these were forgotten. On the globe of the earth
The aquiline-headed Roman, who summed in his one per-
    son the powers and ordered science of humanity,
Stood and possessed his orb of empire, and looked at the
    stars. Then the voice cried
"The pride of the earth."

                        But Vasquez laughed aloud, for
    the earth was a grain of dust circling the fire,
And the fire itself but a spark, among innumerable sparks.
    The swarm of the points of light drifting
No path down darkness merged its pin-prick eyelets into
    one misty glimmer, a mill-stone in shape,
A coin in shape, a mere coin, a flipped luckpenny: but
    again Vasquez
Laughed out, for who was the spendthrift sowed them all
    over the sky, indistinguishable innumerable
Fish-scales of light? They drew together as they drifted
    away no path down the wild darkness; he saw
The webs of their rays made them one tissue, their rays
    that were their very substance and power filled wholly
The space they were in, so that each one touched all, there
    was no division between them, no emptiness, and each
Changed substance with all the others and became the
    others. It was dreadful to see
No space between them, no cave of peace nor no night of
    quietness, no blind spot nor no deaf heart, but the
    tides
Of power and substance flood every cranny; no annihi-
    lation, no escape but change: it must endure itself

Forever. It has the strength to endure itself. We others,
    being faintly made of the dust of a grain of dust
Have been permitted to fool our patience asleep by invent-
    ing death. A poor comfort, he thought,
Yet better than none, the imaginary cavern, how we all
    come clamoring
To the gates of our great invention after few years.
Though a cheat, it works.

                      The speckled tissue of universes
Drew into one formed and rounded light, and Vasquez
Worshiped the one light. One eye ... what, an eye?
A dark mountain with an eye in its cliff? A coal-black
    stallion
Eyed with one burning eye in the mid brow?
Night has an eye. The poor little vision-seer
Groaned, that he never had wit to understand visions.
See all and know nothing. The eye that makes its own light
And sees nothing but itself. "I am seeing Barclay again,"
He marveled, as who should say "I am seeing God:
But what is God?" He continued gazing,
And beads of sweat spilled from his forehead into
    the fire-edge
Ashes. He saw at last, neither the eyed mountain
Nor the stallion, nor Barclay, but his own eye
In the darkness of his own face.

                      The circuit was closed:
"I can endure all things," he thought, "forever. I am he
Whom I have sought.

                  And Clare loves all things
Because all things are herself. She has killed her father
And inherited. Her old enormous father

[*106*]

Who rode the furrows full tilt, sowing with both hands
The high field above the hills and the ocean. We kill steers
    for meat, and God
To be atoned with him. But I remain from myself divided,
    gazing beyond the flaming walls,
Not fortunate enough, and too faint-hearted."

                                        He continued
        gazing across the wane of the fire at the dark
Vision of his own face turned sideways, the light of one
    eye. Clare turned in her place and awoke and said,
"How awfully little. Ooh, Ooh," in a dove's voice,
And then, "I forgot I wasn't alone, Onorio:
And here are the sheep. Have I slept a moment?
I did have a strange dream. I went out across the starlight
Knocking through flight after flight of the shiny balls
And got so far away that the sun and the great earth
And beautiful moon and all the stars were blended
Into one tiny light, Oh terribly little,
The flame of a pitiful little candle blown over
In the wind of darkness, in the fear of the night. It was
    so tiny
I wanted to be its comfort
And hold it and rock it on my breast. One wee flicker
In all the wild dark. What a dream." She turned anxiously
To touch the sheep, fondling their heads and naming them.
"Dear Fay, dear Fern. And here's Captain Saul. Ah bad
    little Hornie
Who taught you to be so bold?" Suddenly she cried
"Did Leader and Frannie go out — did two of the sheep
Go out lately?" But Vasquez, caught in his vision,
Answered "You also have broken
The fire-studded egg of heaven and we're together
In the world outside." "Ah Ah," she cried desolately,

"Did you lie when you counted them? When I was sick
And my eyes failed?" She ran into the darkness outside,
    calling their names;
The flock that remained stood up, in the edge of firelight,
    tremulously crying. Then Vasquez: "I hear a multi-
    tude
Of people crying, but why do you lament and cry? You
    particles of eye of light, if some of you
Endure evil, the others endure good, the balance is perfect.
    The eye lives on mixed light and darkness,
Not either alone. And you are not many but one, the eye
    is not glad nor sorry, nor the dark face
Disquieted: be quiet, voices, and hear the real voice." Clare
    Walker came in from the dark with wide strained eyes,
In each iris the fire reflected made a red stain, and she
    cried:
"Onorio, for Christ's sake tell me, were they not with me?
Or have they slipped out?" He turned slowly an unanswer-
    ing face
Of cool, dark and deaf stone, tempered to the mood
Of what he imagined ... or perhaps perceived. And Clare:
"If I have slept and been dreaming while they're in danger
Or die in the dark: and they cried for me
In the dead night, while I slept and ate: I hope that all
    the miseries I ever feared for myself
Will come doubled, the rain on my hair be knives of ice,
    the sun whips of fire, the death I must die
Drawn out and dreadful like the dream of hell: Onorio,
    Oh come,
Help me to find them!" He rose, passively under com-
    mand in the shrill of her voice, muttering: "I can't
Imagine what further's to find: yet I'll go along.
Is there another light or another darkness?"

"Oh," she answered, "it's black," and snatched the most
    eager brands
Out of the fire for a torch. He with deft fingers
Mimicking her act, but with a sleepwalker mindlessness,
Bound fire into a bundle of sallow twigs,
And calmly, twirling his torch to flame, followed
The red glow of her rod-ends. They ran on the bridge and
    wandered
Up the wet road, Clare calling her flock around her
And sobbing the names of the lost. The useless torches
Flared in the puddles and ruts of water, and ruddied
The plump backs of the sheep; so sanguine-outlined
The little ridiculous procession strayed up the road
In the lane of the trees, the great-trunked wood like storms
Of darkness on either hand. The torches died soon,
Then Clare stood still, desolately calling; weak dawn
Had washed all the world gray.

                            The heads of the little flock
Suddenly and all together were turned one way, then a
    limping ewe
Came out of the wood. Clare screamed with joy, and ran
    and dropped on her knees to embrace the lean neck.
    "Oh Leader!
Leader! She's safe, Onorio. Oh Leader where's Frannie?"
    But then the wound was discovered, the flap torn back
Red from the flank and hanging from the rump, and the
    blood-caked wool. Clare moaned awhile with no words,
    and said,
"When I forgot you because I was sick, when I forgot to
    call you and count you in the rain in the night:
I wish I had died. I have nothing but these,
Onorio, to take care of, and lose and lose. She used to go
    first always, I called her Leader:

And now she's hurt." Onorio heard Clare's teeth clacking
    together in the thin cheeks, and her breath
Hissing between them, he answered calmly, still caught in
    his vision: "The five claws of a lion. Look, Clare.
But don't grieve, the great river of the blood of life is
    always bursting its banks, never runs dry,
Secret inexhaustible fountains feed it." She stared at his
    face and turned on the forest her desert eyes
And wrung her hands. "Leader is hurt; and Frannie I think
    has died."

                They searched long; the fourth hour
Of daylight they found the half consumed body. The head
    was not mangled, Clare fell beside it
On the wet earth and kissed the half open eyes,
Weeping and self-reproachful, but yet she lamented
Less violently than Vasquez had feared. At length
He said, "If you wish, Clare, I will fetch tools
And bury it here." She answered faintly, "No matter.
She feels nothing to-day, darkness nor light,
Teeth nor the grave. Oh, I loved her well: but now, see,
She's not living any more. Onorio ... isn't that your name?
What a stately name! ... this is the one that fed me
    with milk
Long after the others were dry, she was like a mother to
    me, when I might have starved.
She loved me, I know.
But even the udders are torn. Her name, Onorio, was
    Frannie."
She turned and said, "Poor Leader. Can you come now?
Come Fern, come Fay, come Tiny, we have to go on.
Come Saul."

              Vasquez begged her to turn again
And stay at his father's place in the canyon

Until she was well. She had to go on, she answered.

And Vasquez: "My father is withered up with old age
   but he'd be kind; and my brothers
Would be your brothers. There's pasture for the sheep.
   We're only a sort of Indians but we can be kind.
   Come, Clare.
The place is pleasant and alone, up the deep canyon,
   beside the old quarry and the kilns where they burnt
   the lime.
A hundred laborers used to live there, but now the woods
   have grown back, the cabins are standing empty,
The roads are gone. I think the old masonry kilns are
   beautiful, standing like towers in the deep forest,
But cracked and leaning, and maidenhair fern grows
   from the cracks. The creek makes music below. Come,
   Clare.
It is deep with peace. When I have to go about and work
   on men's farms for wages I long for that place
Like some one thinking of water in deserts. Sometimes we
   hear the sea's thunder, far down the deep gorge.
The darkness under the trees in spring is starry with
   flowers, with redwood sorrel, colt's foot, wakerobin,
The slender-stemmed pale yellow violets,
And Solomon's seal that makes intense islands of fragrance
   in April." "Oh, April," she said trembling,
"How exactly it follows. How could I rest? Ah, no,
Good-by, good-by, Onorio. Poor Leader, I am sure
We can go a little way before dark. Come, Saul, Saul."
She ran a few steps, panting hard.

                              Vasquez perceived
No hope of staying her: "Then I'll go back to the bridge
And fetch my horse and my coat. I'll not leave you, Clare."
He went slowly, heavy and amazed. His horse

Had broken tether in the night, stung by the hail-stones.
Then Vasquez, still drunken with the dregs of his vision
To fatalist indifference, went hunting the horse
And found it late. He followed Clare the next morning,
But met another vision on the road, that waved
Impatient white hands against his passage, saying
"If I go up to Calvary ten million times: what is that to
    you?
Let me go up." Vasquez drew rein and sat staring.
He saw beyond the vision in the yellow mud
Prints of bare feet, dibbled about with many
Little crowding hoof-marks; he marveled, feeling no sad-
    ness
But lonely thoughts.

XII

                      Clare Walker had crossed the ridge
    and gone down
To the mouth of Cawdor's Canyon. Japanese tenants
Now kept the house; short broad-faced men who planted
Lettuces in the garden against the creek-side
And beans on the hill. The barns were vacant, the cattle
Were vanished from the high pastures. The men were
    friendly,
Clare begged at their hands a little oil to soften
The bandage on Leader's wound; she'd torn her spent
    dress
In strips to bind it, and went now without clothing
But the long brown cloak.

                      She went northward, and on a
    foreland
Found vacant cabins around a ruined saw-mill;

And finding sacks of dry straw with a worn blanket
In one of the cabins, slept well and awoke refreshed
To travel on slowly northward in the glad sunlight
And sparkle of the sea. But the next day was dark,
And one of the wethers died, she never knew why,
She wept and went on.

                Near Point Lobos, by a gate
Where Tamar Cauldwell used to lean from her white pony
To swing the bars, the lion-stricken ewe, Leader,
Groaned and.lay down and died. Clare met much kindness
    there;
She was nursed in the house, helpless, for many days,
And the sheep were guarded and fed. The people clothed
    her
And calmed her wild mind; but she was not willing to tell
    them
Her griefs nor her cause of fear. They kept her by watch-
    ful force
Until she escaped, a great night of moonlight, and fled
With her small flock.

                Far up the Carmel Valley
The river became a brook, she watched a salmon
Row its worn body up-stream over the stones
And struck by a thwart current expose the bruised
White belly to the white of the sky, gashed with red
    wounds, but right itself
And wriggle up-stream, having that within it, spirit or
    desire,
Will spend all its dear flesh and all the power it has gath-
    ered, in the sweet salt pastures and fostering ocean,
To find the appointed high-place and perish. Clare Walker,
    in a bright moment's passage of anxious feeling,

Knowing nothing of its fate saw her own fate reflected.
　She drank, and the sheep drank; they went up the valley
And crossed, the next day, among the long-needled pines,
　the great thirsty sky-ridge.

　　　　　　　　　In the valley beyond
Clare journeyed northward again, anxiously avoiding
The traveled roads and hiding herself from people
In fear that some one's force or kindness might steal her
From the helpless flock; and later in habitual fear.

She was seen much later, heavily swollen
Toward child-birth, cowering from a thin April rain
By a little fire on the San Joaquin river-bank,
Sharing a camp of outcast men; no sheep
Remained with her, but when she moved in the morning
She called the names of many, Fern, Fay and Leader,
Nosie and Saul and little Hornie and the others,
"Dear Tiny, dear Frannie, come on, we have to go on."
The toothless tramp bandaging his foot by the fire
Looked up with a flicker of light in his slack face,
And the sickly sullen boy on the other side
Smiled without mockery. Clare had gone half a mile
And felt a grinding pang in her back, she clung to the fence
And saw the poplars planted along the road
Reach dreadfully away northward. When the pain ended
She went on northward; but after the second pain
She crept down to the river and hid her body
In a willow thicket. In the evening, between the rapid
Summits of agony before exhaustion, she called
The sheep about her and perceived that none came.

THE BROKEN BALANCE

I

REFERENCE
TO A PASSAGE IN PLUTARCH'S
LIFE OF SULLA

THE people buying and selling, consuming pleasures,
    talking in the archways,
Were all suddenly struck quiet
And ran from under stone to look up at the sky: so shrill
    and mournful,
So fierce and final, a brazen
Pealing of trumpets high up in the air, in the summer blue
    over Tuscany.
They marveled; the soothsayers answered:
"Although the Gods are little troubled toward men, at the
    end of each period
A sign is declared in heaven
Indicating new times, new customs, a changed people; the
    Romans
Rule, and Etruria is finished;
A wise mariner will trim the sails to the wind."

                    I heard yesterday
So shrill and mournful a trumpet-blast,
It was hard to be wise.... You must eat change and en-
    dure; not be much troubled

For the people; they will have their happiness.
When the republic grows too heavy to endure, then Cæsar
    will carry it;
When life grows hateful, there's power . . .

II

TO THE CHILDREN

Power's good; life is not always good but power's good.
So you must think when abundance
Makes pawns of people and all the loaves are one dough.
The steep singleness of passion
Dies; they will say, "What was that?" but the power
    triumphs.
Loveliness will live under glass
And beauty will go savage in the secret mountains.
There is beauty in power also.
You children must widen your minds' eyes to take moun-
    tains
Instead of faces, and millions
Instead of persons; not to hate life; and massed power
After the lone hawk's dead.

III

That light blood-loving weasel, a tongue of yellow
Fire licking the sides of the gray stones,
Has a more passionate and more pure heart
In the snake-slender flanks than man can imagine;
But he is betrayed by his own courage,
The man who kills him is like a cloud hiding a star.

Then praise the jewel-eyed hawk and the tall blue heron;
The black cormorants that fatten their sea-rock
With shining slime; even that ruiner of anthills
The red-shafted woodpecker flying,
A white star between blood-color wing-clouds,
Across the glades of the wood and the green lakes of shade.

These live their felt natures; they know their norm
And live it to the brim; they understand life.
While men molding themselves to the anthill have choked
Their natures until the souls die in them;
They have sold themselves for toys and protection:
No, but consider awhile: what else? Men sold for toys.

Uneasy and fractional people, having no center
But in the eyes and mouths that surround them,
Having no function but to serve and support
Civilization, the enemy of man,
No wonder they live insanely, and desire
With their tongues, progress; with their eyes, pleasure;
      with their hearts, death.

Their ancestors were good hunters, good herdsmen and
      swordsmen,
But now the world is turned upside down;
The good do evil, the hope's in criminals; in vice
That dissolves the cities and war to destroy them.
Through wars and corruptions the house will fall.
Mourn whom it falls on. Be glad: the house is mined, it
      will fall.

IV

Rain, hail and brutal sun, the plow in the roots,
The pitiless pruning-iron in the branches,

Strengthen the vines, they are all feeding friends
Or powerless foes until the grapes purple.
But when you have ripened your berries it is time to begin
    to perish.

The world sickens with change, rain becomes poison,
The earth is a pit, it is time to perish.
The vines are fey, the very kindness of nature
Corrupts what her cruelty before strengthened.
When you stand on the peak of time it is time to begin to
    perish.

Reach down the long morbid roots that forget the plow,
Discover the depths; let the long pale tendrils
Spend all to discover the sky, now nothing is good
But only the steel mirrors of discovery . . .
And the beautiful enormous dawns of time, after we perish.

V

Mourning the broken balance, the hopeless prostration of
    the earth
Under men's hands and their minds,
The beautiful places killed like rabbits to make a city,
The spreading fungus, the slime-threads
And spores; my own coast's obscene future: I remember
    the farther
Future, and the last man dying
Without succession under the confident eyes of the stars.
It was only a moment's accident,
The race that plagued us; the world resumes the old lonely
    immortal
Splendor; from here I can even

Perceive that that snuffed candle had something . . . a fantastic virtue,
A faint and unshapely pathos . . .
So death will flatter them at last: what, even the bald ape's by-shot
Was moderately admirable?

VI

PALINODE

All summer neither rain nor wave washes the cormorants'
Perch, and their droppings have painted it shining white.
If the excrement of fish-eaters makes the brown rock a snow-mountain
At noon, a rose in the morning, a beacon at moonrise
On the black water: it is barely possible that even men's present
Lives are something; their arts and sciences (by moonlight)
Not wholly ridiculous, nor their cities merely an offense.

VII

Under my windows, between the road and the sea-cliff, bitter wild grass
Stands narrowed between the people and the storm.
The ocean winter after winter gnaws at its earth, the wheels and the feet
Summer after summer encroach and destroy.
Stubborn green life, for the cliff-eater I cannot comfort you, ignorant which color,

Gray-blue or pale-green, will please the late stars;
But laugh at the other, your seed shall enjoy wonderful
vengeances and suck
The arteries and walk in triumph on the faces.

BIRTH=DUES

JOY is a trick in the air; pleasure is merely contemptible,
 the dangled
Carrot the ass follows to market or precipice;
But limitary pain — the rock under the tower and the hewn
 coping
That takes thunder at the head of the turret —
Terrible and real. Therefore a mindless dervish carving
 himself
With knives will seem to have conquered the world.

The world's God is treacherous and full of unreason; a
 torturer, but also
The only foundation and the only fountain.
Who fights him eats his own flesh and perishes of hunger;
 who hides in the grave
To escape him is dead; who enters the Indian
Recession to escape him is dead; who falls in love with the
 God is washed clean
Of death desired and of death dreaded.

He has joy, but joy is a trick in the air; and pleasure, but
 pleasure is contemptible;
And peace; and is based on solider than pain.
He has broken boundaries a little and that will estrange
 him; he is monstrous, but not
To the measure of the God. . . . But I having told you —
However I suppose that few in the world have energy to
 hear effectively —
Have paid my birth-dues; am quits with the people.

THE HUMANIST'S TRAGEDY

NOT like a beast borne on the flood of passion, boat
    without oars, but mindful of all his dignity
As human being, a king and a Greek, King Pentheus: "Tell
    him that we will reverence the Gods we have,
But not minded to increase the burden. What new ones
    ship raging like beasts from Asia by the islands
We've whips for, here in Thebes. Tell him to take his
    magic-drunken women and be off." The messenger
Went up to the mountain wood; needles of pine stuck in the
    sandal-straps of the man returning
At noon and saying: "He could not hear me, O King. I
    shouted aloud, clothed in the king's authority,
Showing him the wand I carried: the God's ... I say the
    stranger's ... eyes like blue ice looked through my
    body
As if I had been an open window in the breast of a wall.
    He bored through me toward Thebes and answered
Not me, the raging laughing women: 'They have Isemenus
    to drink of, and Dirce, and all the fountains,
Must they have wine too?' What more he said, my lord, I
    cannot remember. But I, having seen more
Than I dare tell, turned home." "Ten spearmen," the king
    answered, biting the bearded lip, "will do it.
What more saw you? Dread not to tell, obscene or magic.
    We are master of ourself as of this people.
Not like a beast borne on the flood of passion, boat without
    oars, but mindful of all our dignity
As human being, a king and a Greek: no random lightning
    of anger will stab the messenger. We're sane still

[*122*]

Though the air swarms." The messenger: "My lord, my
    lord..." And the king: "Out with it." "The lady
    Agave, my lord."
"Our mother," the king answered frowning. "— Was in the
    mountain with the other women, dancing, adoring."
King Pentheus' knuckles, of the hand that held the long
Smooth-shaven staff tipped with the head of a man carved
    in pale ivory, whitened, and the hand reddened
Under the scant stipple of black hair. More than that was
    no motion. "Well, she was in the mountain,"
He answered, "My mother was there," the king housing
    his wrath in hard self-mastery. He had the chariot
Horsed, and rode swiftly toward Cythaeron; the glens and
    the slope bristled with forest. In a glade he found
    them.
He had come alone; the charioteer stayed by the sweating
    horses. Without awe, without pleasure,
As a man spies on noxious beasts, he standing hidden spied
    on the rabid choir of the God.
They had pine-cone-tipped wands, they went half naked,
    they were hoarse with insane song; foam from their
    mouths, mingled
With wine and sweat, ran down their bodies. O fools, boats
    without oars borne on the flood of passion,
Forgetting utterly all the dignity of man, the pride of the
    only self-commanding animal,
That captains his own soul and controls even
Fate, for a space. The only animal that turns means to an
    end. "What end? Oh, but what end?"
It cried under his mind, "Increase the city? subdue the
    earth? Breed slaves and cattle, and one's own
Off-shots, fed and secure? Ah fruitful-fruitless
Generations forever and ever.... For pleasure"— he spat
    on the earth —"the slight collectible pleasure

Surplus to pain?" Then recollecting all his dignity as
    human being, a king and a Greek,
He heard with hostile ears the hoarse and beastlike choir
    of the worshipers: "O sisters, we have found an
    opening,
We have hewn in the stone and mortar
A wild strait gateway,
Slit eyes in the mask, sisters,
Entered the mountain.
We shall be sad to-morrow when the wine dies,
The God dies from our blood;
To-day in the forest
We are fire and have found an opening."
His own mother Agave singing. Endure a little. If one
    could understand their fountain
Of madness. Her shame to-morrow: not punishment
    enough: prison in the house. "O sisters, we have found
    an opening:"
What opening?

                    The boys from Thebes to be whipped, the
    Theban women shut up a fortnight, the God and his
    Thracian
Satyrs and women ... "The generations," he thought sud-
    denly, "aspire. They better; they climb; as I
Am better than this weak suggestible woman my mother.
    Had I forgotten a moment the end
Of being? To increase the power, collectedness and dignity
    of man.— A more collected and dignified
Creature," he groaned, "to die and stink."

                    That moment like a tall ship
    breasting through water the God

[*124*]

Passed, the high head, the shining hair and the blond
    shoulders, trailing a wake of ecstasy like foam
Across the multitude of faces like waves, his frantic wor-
    shipers. He anchored among them smiling
In the wild midst, and said softly: "When you are dead
    you become part of peace; let no man
Dream more of death; there is neither sight nor hearing
    nor any wonder; none of us Gods enters it.
You become part of peace, part of the sacred beauty, but
    having no part: as if a flute-player
Should make beauty but hear none, being deaf and sense-
    less. But living if you will
It is possible for you to break prison of yourselves and
    enter the nature of things and use the beauty.
Wine and lawlessness, art and music, love, self-torture,
    religion,
Are means but are not needful, contemplation will do it.
    Only to break human collectedness.
The least shepherd on Cythaeron, if he dares, might do it.
    But you being neophyte all, Thracians and Thebans,
Are indeed somewhat wild, somewhat too drunken."

                          King Pentheus then, seeing
    his enemy, but ever
Stately mindful of all his dignity, as human being, a king
    and a Greek, entered among them
Angrily to fetch his mother. Agave cried out,
"Sisters: a lion stalking us, a wild beast of the pinewood,
    or is it a wolf?" She leading eagerly,
Full of the courage that the God had taught them, rushed
    on her son not known, and the others raging
Joined her; the frantic voices, the tearing fingers, the teeth
    and the madness...

The God and his people went down
Toward Thebes, Agave dancing before them, the head of
    her son the triumph in her hands, the beard and the
    blood:
"A lion I have killed in the mountain,
Thebans, the head of a lion my own hands hunted,
With my hands, a lion!"

EVENING EBB

THE ocean has not been so quiet for a long while; five
    night-herons
Fly shorelong voiceless in the hush of the air
Over the calm of an ebb that almost mirrors their wings.
The sun has gone down, and the water has gone down
From the weed-clad rock, but the distant cloud-wall rises.
    The ebb whispers.
Great cloud-shadows float in the opal water.
Through rifts in the screen of the world pale gold gleams,
    and the evening
Star suddenly glides like a flying torch.
As if we had not been meant to see her; rehearsing behind
The screen of the world for another audience.

HANDS

INSIDE a cave in a narrow canyon near Tassajara
The vault of rock is painted with hands,
A multitude of hands in the twilight, a cloud of men's
    palms, no more,
No other picture. There's no one to say
Whether the brown shy quiet people who are dead intended
Religion or magic, or made their tracings
In the idleness of art; but over the division of years these
    careful
Signs-manual are now like a sealed message
Saying: "Look: we also were human; we had hands, not
    paws. All hail
You people with the cleverer hands, our supplanters
In the beautiful country; enjoy her a season, her beauty,
    and come down
And be supplanted; for you also are human."

HOODED NIGHT

AT night, toward dawn, all the lights of the shore have
   died,
And a wind moves. Moves in the dark
The sleeping power of the ocean, no more beastlike than
   manlike,
Not to be compared; itself and itself.
Its breath blown shoreward huddles the world with a fog;
   no stars
Dance in heaven; no ship's light glances.
I see the heavy granite bodies of the rocks of the headland,
That were ancient here before Egypt had pyramids,
Bulk on the gray of the sky, and beyond them the jets of
   young trees
I planted the year of the Versailles peace.
But here is the final unridiculous peace. Before the first
   man
Here were the stones, the ocean, the cypresses,
And the pallid region in the stone-rough dome of fog where
   the moon
Falls on the west. Here is reality.
The other is a spectral episode: after the inquisitive
   animal's
Amusements are quiet: the dark glory.

AFTERWORD

ALTHOUGH the son of an austere Presbyterian minister and seminary professor, Robinson Jeffers had renounced Christianity long before entering upon his mature poetic career. He therefore looked on Jesus as a divine figure only in the mythic sense, that is, either as a momentary revelation of his pantheistic god, as described, for instance, in *Roan Stallion,* or as an archetypal manifestation of the cyclic death-resurrection pattern which is the Life of the World, as dramatized in "At the Birth of an Age." At the same time, Jeffers did find Jesus a challenging and pivotal historical figure with whom he must necessarily contend when analyzing the dynamics of Western thought and piety.

The present volume, *Dear Judas and Other Poems,*[1] reveals Jeffers coming to grips with the Jesus phenomenon from a number of angles. *Dear Judas* and *The Loving Shepherdess* are companion pieces. In the first, Jesus is a

1. *Dear Judas* was the fourth Jeffers publication to be issued by Liveright, being preceded by *Roan Stallion and Other Poems* (1925), *The Women at Point Sur* (1927), and *Cawdor and Other Poems* (1928). *Tamar and Other Poems,* a dramatic departure from his earlier volumes, *Flagons and Apples* (1912) and *Californians* (1916), had been published by Peter Boyle in 1924. Neglected and all but forgotten, it was picked up almost a year later by critics James Rorty, Mark Van Doren, and Babette Deutsch. Their enthusiasm rocketed Jeffers into notoriety and critical acceptance.

charismatic young man, anguished over the identity of his father, who is led by circumstances and by an inner dialectic toward power to choose a two-thousand-year possession of men's hearts at the price of painful crucifixion. Clare Walker, his Good Shepherd figure, explores another aspect of the Jesus phenomenon, the savior complex, which Jeffers found to be the most insidious and seductive syndrome to attack men of good will.

Jeffers' original intent was to call the volume "The Gentle Shepherdess and Other Poems." The shepherdess tale, he tells us, is the "story of one who has committed self-sacrifice . . . a saint, I suppose, going to a natural martyrdom, aureoled with such embellishments as the mind of time permits." Regarding his passion play, *Dear Judas,* he reflects: "It seems to me to present, in a somewhat new dramatic form, new and probable explanations of the mythical characters and acts of its protagonists." Jeffers sees a special relationship between the two longer narratives of the book: "The shepherdess in the one and Judas and Jesus in the other, each embodying different aspects of love: nearly pure, therefore undefiled but quite inefficient in the first; pitying in the second; possessive in the third."[2]

From its inception, *Dear Judas* had a turbulent history. It precipitated the enduring wrath of Yvor Winters, an attack from which Jeffers' reputation was never fully to recover.[3] Although a dramatic *tour de force,* the play was

2. Sidney Alberts, *A Bibliography of the Works of Robinson Jeffers* (New York, 1933), pp. 56–57.

3. Yvor Winters, "Robinson Jeffers," *Poetry,* 35 (Feb., 1930), 279–286. Reprinted in Zabel, *Literary Opinion in America* (New York, 1937), pp. 439–493. "Mr. Jeffers' mouthpiece and hero, Jesus, is a little short of revolting as he whips reflexively from didactic passion to malice, self-justification and vengeance. The poem shares the structural prnciples, or lack of them, of *The Women at Point Sur;* and it has no quotable lines, save possibly

excluded from Jeffers' *Selected Poetry* (1938), not entirely because of space considerations. As a theater presentation it fared even worse. In the late 1940s it was adapted for the stage by Eric Vaughn for a premiere in Oakland, California — only to be suppressed by a bishop's threat of excommunication against two of its principal players and its choreographer. In 1947 it was produced on the East Coast with Bach chorales and interpretive dance in an adaptation by Michael Myerberg, who had successfully presented Thornton Wilder's *The Skin of Our Teeth*. Myerberg had intended the premiere to be in Boston, but churchmen objected so vociferously that Mayor John Hynes and the city censor, Walter Milliken, warned against it. In his public statement, the mayor cautioned that the play would "violate the beliefs of many Bostonians in God and might even create trouble by stirring religious feeling." Subsequently, despite fierce opposition mounted by a prominent Catholic layman, *Dear Judas* opened on August 4 in the Playhouse of Ogunquit, Maine, to a "small and enthusiastic audience." It was then scheduled for a major opening in New York on October 5. For this opening Jeffers was persuaded to write a presentation essay for the New York *Times* to clarify his poetic intent.

Jeffers began his essay with an analysis of his audience expectations. "It was not written for the stage; the thoughts and attitudes it presents are not those that would be expected by any probable audience and people are bewildered or repelled by what is strange to them. If they come to see

---

the last three, which are, however, heavy with dross." *The Loving Shepherdess* "succeeds in being no more than a very Wordsworthian embodiment of a kind of maudlin humanitarianism." See Alex Vardamis, *The Critical Reputation of Robinson Jeffers: A Bibliographical Study* (Hamden, Conn., 1972), pp. 71–79, for a summary of the reviews on *Dear Judas*.

a passion play, I thought, they expect either chromo or technicolor sentimentality; but *Dear Judas* needs some quickness of intelligence to be understood at all."[4] Following this opening, Jeffers registered his amazement at "the absurdities of boycott and prohibition" which the play had met with and added, "This is the first time, so far as I know, that the [Boston] 'banning' has been not on a moral but frankly a theological basis. It is ridiculous and I suppose illegal." The author then reaffirmed that the play was not written out of any desire to disturb religious faith but merely to express the great passions that have so significantly moved the world's history. He had chosen the Noh genre in order to avoid the hazards of depicting the passions and persons directly. Ever since his early attentive reading of the Gospels, "under the stern eye of the Presbyterian clergyman, my father," Jeffers had been intrigued by the simplicity of the deeds and sayings as set against the "complexity of the minds." "The mind of Jesus is shown to us as if unintentionally, in wonderful glimpses through the objective narration. It is deep, powerful and beautiful and strangely complex, not wholly integrated." Here, says Jeffers, is not the mind of merely incarnated love, but of a man of genius, a poet and a leader who grips twenty centuries and forms "the greatest age of human history." Hesitating to depict this mind directly, he has represented it through "its ghost; its echo or afterflame." Regarding the mind of Judas, Jeffers would caution us that the Gospels reveal even less; this mind comes to us "obscure and sick and divided"; it may be either tragic

4. This and the subsequent quotations in this paragraph are from the New York *Times,* Oct. 5, 1947, sec. 2, p. 1. Reprinted in Melba Bennett, *The Stone Mason of Tor House* (Los Angeles, 1966), pp. 196–198.

or reptilian, depending on what we presume drives it. Jeffers chooses to interpret Judas as "skeptical, humanitarian, pessimistic and sick with pity."

Jeffers' *Times* article evidently convinced few. The public was not yet ready for what seems to have been a very sensitive and richly artful production. Myerberg's New York run lasted a scant two weeks. It does seem unfortunate that the staged *Dear Judas* was never afforded more serious professional scrutiny. Whatever its artistic shortcomings, it has at various times provided stunning spectacle and challenging drama, but only by small troupes such as the Interplayers of San Francisco. The theme and handling no longer appear calculated to offend Christian sensitivities—which today seem more tolerant of such interpretations or of the artist's right to make them. The play can be viewed as sacrilegious only in the sense that it does not witness the orthodox belief in the sacred, central, and redemptive character of Jesus' passion, but views the Christ-event in light of possible psychological and sociological readings. If the play desecrates, this is only because Jeffers sees the sacred coming from a different quarter. A deeply religious respect for the divine, wherever it be manifest, is characteristic of Jeffers' life and poetry.

Though introduced to the West with some flourish by Ernest Fenollosa, Ezra Pound, and William Butler Yeats, the Noh play form is unusual to the American drama scene. Noh is a fourteenth-century Japanese ritualistic drama — combining dance, high diction, music, masks, and formal conventions of staging and plot development. The participants act out, in a recurring, purgatorial fashion, the passionate connection they have with the place (here the Garden of Gethsemane) to which they are drawn in order to relive the past. They revisit their death struggle, their underworld experience, and the longing they have for release. For a time unspecified, they are chained by earthly passions which bind them to the world of actuality and withhold from them the attainment of peace.

The Noh patterns fit well into Jeffers' dramaturgy. In Noh plays, the scene is central; Jeffers called landscape his "seed-plot"; he first felt the *place* and then invented human characters to express its mood.[5] The Noh action is ritualistic; movement is slow, a basic rhythm being established by drum and flute and by a chorus of men chanting the narrative parts. Jeffers' poetic concern was pervasively ritualistic — seeking to attune his reader and himself to the underlying patterns of death and rebirth. Ghosts or apparitions are common in Jeffers' dramas and lyrics. A materialist, believing only in this world of existence and eschewing all spiritual dimensions, he still uses ghosts as a very effective dramatic strategy — sometimes as a personification of eddying currents of energy, carrying the world toward a fiery culmination as in *Tamar;* sometimes as doppelgängers, embodying the psychological split in the *dramatis personae* as in *Mara;* sometimes as residual presences or after-images, slowly dissipating their energies, such as those found in "Post Mortem" and in the opening of *Dear Judas.*

The character development in Jeffers' play follows the Noh pattern, although Jeffers adapts this convention in his own unique ways. Noh characters undergo metamorphoses — a passionate, deceived woman, explaining her fate, later appears as a young girl, innocent of her future. Noh time

5. See Jeffers' Preface to Horace Lyon's *Jeffers Country* (San Francisco, 1971), p. 10. See also Jeffers' *Selected Letters* (Baltimore, 1968), No. 231.

is fluid, not chronological but causal and associational. In this vein, Jeffers' Mary appears first as a disillusioned and bitter crone, singing her "cracked song," then as Mother Night, detached, distant, a philosophic observer asking, "Do you still have saviors?" and noting the net of determinism in which all are caught, and then finally as the troubled, possessive, delusion-obsessed mother who resists the truth of the cross. The development of the Jesus character, on the other hand, is almost linear. Jesus is successively a bright, intriguing prophet; a would-be earthly king; an angry, crowd-provoked rebel; a calculating manipulator of the violence which wins men's hearts; a mystic visionary, seeing all things in the overview of divine necessity; and a transcendentally cynical possessor of two thousand years' homage through his self-inflicted martyrdom.

Jeffers' use of the Scriptures is fascinating and provocative. He does some violence to the evangelists' figure of Jesus; yet the moments he invokes have their credibility. They are drawn from the unexplained, enigmatic episodes of the Gospels — Jesus' rejection of his mother, his violence in the temple, his threats to destroy, his choleric blasting of the unoffending fig tree, his apocalyptic warnings. Jeffers does little to distort the actual quotation; often the dialogue disconcertingly reappears word for word from the Gospel. However, he changes the setting and telescopes incidents and selectively screens out what does not further his interpretation.

Though the action is continuous, the play has three divisions: Judas' dream (pp. 10–28), Jesus' dream (pp. 29–39), and Mary's dream (pp. 39–49) — derived from the "three remnant images of three passions too violent to vanish." These divisions, though not formally marked off, are indicated by a shift in point of view — from Judas to

Jesus to Mary — and by the removal of the previous actor-in-focus from the stage.[6]

The first "act" belongs to Judas. After an opening scene which functions as introduction and point of entry, Jesus turns the action over to him ("Since you must dream, dream on from there"). Judas then relives his first meeting with the Master, confessing to him the exquisite sensitivity which is to be his downfall, and receiving from him in turn Jesus' confession of his own torture concerning his father's identity which is his driving obsession. The catastrophe inherent in the confluence of these sensitivities is prefigured in troubling "black shadows that move/Immeasurably stretched on the white road [that] seem to reach even to Jerusalem." Judas hears Mother Night's scathing pronouncement against saviors in answer to his delusions of Jesus' power and is disturbed by her invocation of the "torches of violence" that must move their world toward its culmination. Mother Night recapitulates for him Jesus' growing ambition, which has reached the point of fomenting rebellion and grasping at kingship. Judas is then confronted by a disturbing parable, his memory of Peter's casual cruelty in winging a hawk. "It will trail pain till it starves" but "its wound saves many sparrows." This incident symbolizes his dilemma over the Master: Jesus is the hawk; men are the birds to be spared. Jesus' ironic delusions of being lifted up and of standing on a high tower (prefiguring his crucifixion) bring Jesus openly to invite a showdown in Jerusalem (pp. 18–20). Following a soliloquy by Mary, now the naïve, doting mother, Judas

6. Eric Vaughn, in an unpublished paper, "'Dear Judas': Time and the Dramatic Structure of the Dream" (Bowling Green, 1976), charts fifty-six time phases through which the play moves — thirty-two in the first part, eighteen in the second, and six in the third.

[*138*]

returns from Jerusalem with the powerful speech "the glory is departed" (pp. 22–24) in which he details with horror the dreadful changes in his Master, precipitated by the collapse of his regal ambitions. Begun in petulance, Jesus' violent acts and speeches have proved to be a weapon of power, "the dreadful key to their hearts." Judas now sees clearly his duty and destiny. After an exchange with Jesus' mother in which revulsion, homage, and self-recrimination mix, Judas enters into his final delusion — that he can be savior of Jesus and of his people by having Jesus put under restraint for three or four days. It is at this point, as Judas passes heavily from center stage, that the second dream begins, that of Jesus himself.

Jesus is more perceptive than Judas of the nature of the "dream" that is both his recurring passion and, in breathtakingly broader circles, the life of the world. As though expanding on Mary's meditation regarding the self-delusion of freedom and responsibility within the netted determinism of life's dream (p. 12), Jesus has observed, "Dreams are deceivers [but] no one's exempt from dreaming, not even I ... fragments of thought fitting themselves together without a mind." Not without a sense of ironic ambiguity, Jesus has pronounced that it is dreadful "to serve the triumphant occasions of God" (p. 19). Now, in the midst of his exultation over the power he wields, manipulating his followers and even Judas to his own ends, Jesus pauses to reflect on the beauty of God who is both night and day, large and small, flourishing and waste, sheep and wolves, beginning and end, "all, all, and time future and past, the hanging leaves on one tree" (p. 22). No single dream declares His loveliness; one cannot speak, only *be* His beauty; all things, including Judas' guilt, are redeemed in this exultant truth. For a moment, like Tamar, Jesus seems to *accept* his role rather than *need* it. What Jeffers has written elsewhere of Woodrow Wilson's savior-delusion can be applied here to Jesus: "Your tragic quality required the huge delusion of some major purpose to produce it." So also can the choral pronouncement in "Margrave": "It is likely the enormous/ Beauty of the world requires for completion our ghostly increment,/It has to dream, and dream badly, a moment of its night." These are all God's dreams.[7]

While moving toward possession of "two thousand years . . . laid in my hands like grains of corn" (p. 32), Jesus acknowledges, along with the monstrosity of his deed ("love run to lust"), its inevitability. The cross is a very "idol of life" and a "power in the dreaming soul of the world" (p. 33).[8] Judas' last plea for restraint is met with words of comfort for the future: all are caught in the net of God's will — a truth that should enable all to endure (p. 36). Orchestrating the action by a call to his disciples for resistance at sword point, Jesus reflects that conquest

7. See "Woodrow Wilson" and "Margrave" in *The Selected Poetry of Robinson Jeffers* (New York, 1938), pp. 172, 371. Dream imagery is thematic in Jeffers' poetry. Dream seems to imply the irrational and nightmare quality of life ("Apology for Bad Dreams"). It can also symbolize the associative mode of his pantheistic god's "discovery" process which utilizes men's lives and passions (*The Beginning and the End,* pp. 9–10). Men, he says, are God's "sense organs"; men's dreams are part of God's dream. Thus the dream concept transcends the Noh convention.

8. This is an axiom of Jeffers' metaphysics, most graphically enunciated in "Apology for Bad Dreams," Jeffers' *ars poetica* and *apologia pro vita sua.* To fulfill its dynamism, Being must be accompanied by waves of violence, since all forms resist change and their matter must be wrested from them to be possessed by new forms. Jeffers dramatizes this powerfully in "At the Birth of an Age" (*Selected Poetry,* p. 560). The cross is symbol ("idol") of the pain and restraint and clashing of opposites which epitomize all life and being.

of Rome by his cross is pure "delirium." Again he com-
forts Judas with his newfound metaphysics of necessary
violence: "All power crushes its object." Therefore, Jesus
is as guilty as Judas. It is really Jesus who sacrifices Judas,
not vice versa. No action and every action is innocent
(p. 37).

For a moment Jesus is tempted to justify his monstrous
act toward the future by the fantasy that he is bringing
mankind closer, in action and perception, to the universal
god; but he must renounce this also as "dreams, dreams."
Rather, all things are amoral; at least, "Who can pick out
the good from the evil?" (p. 38). Jesus closes his dream
with a reassertion of the determinism that exculpates them
all:

> Dear Judas, it is God drives us.
> It is not shameful to be duped by God. I have known
> > his glory in my lifetime, I have *been* his glory,
> > I know
> Beyond illusion the enormous beauty of the torch in
> > which our agonies and all are particles of fire
> > [p. 39].

Mary's dream, the final section, constitutes the denoue-
ment. Exulting over her role in her son's supposed earthly
glorification, she voices her "Magnificat" (compare Luke
1:46–55). In contrast to the clarity of Jesus' dream, Mary's
dream is filled with dramatic irony. Each report from the
passing messengers of calamity is either rejected outright
or twisted into good news — her son is exalted on a hill,
people flock to his feet, he is called their king. As though
outside the action entirely, Lazarus functions as counter to
her delusions. Returned from the dead, he has no dreams,
no emotions to be fulfilled. In effect, he is the play's final

word. Sent every night to tell Mary not to rejoice, he is reconciled to his role, yet reflects that "it would be better for these three/If they could sleep; but the great passions [which] life was not wide enough for are not so easily exhausted,/But echo in the wood for certain years or millenniums" (p. 42). Lazarus as messenger is a mockery of Luke's angel of Annunciation: "Hail Mary, chosen for extremes, remember that grief and happiness are only shadows of a shadow." Lazarus' message continues: "He is hanged on a cross on Golgotha." It is too much for Mary. In vain he urges her that peace is possible only through pressing the truth to her breast and thus conquering life — letting the "smoky unserviceable remainders of love and desire . . . be dissolved and be still" (p. 44). Mary can only turn away and curse the despairing Judas, who enters, lost in a welter of false explanations for his guilty act. Mary goes out toward the bitter enlightenment of the cross; Judas goes to the wood to hang himself; Lazarus is left to conclude the play: the two tree-hanged victims at either pole of the wood are to praise God "after the monstrous manner of mankind."

Here then is Jeffers' passion play. The message has been articulated: men are God's dupes, their lives being God's dreams; each cycle of history is a variation on a theme; history's ruthless agents of power are necessary to move their age's cycle; men are doomed to suffer delusion but truth is available; guilt is ultimately meaningless; God is glorified in all. Jeffers' interwoven themes are familiar ones: that Being aches for annihilation; that cruel and kind, good and evil, are all of a mesh; that all things are determined; that saviorism is illusion; that power is good in that it advances God's self-discovery; that men are blind (faith is willful blindness); that evil is partial vision; that love is a trap; that violence sparks beauty; that pain is inescapable; that religions are tyrannous; that God is inhuman, indifferent, unmerciful, and entirely to be praised.

The Loving Shepherdess, tandem poem to *Dear Judas,* after which the volume was to have been titled, offers a quite different characterization of Jesus. Clare Walker is in many ways a duplicate of the Judas who is doppelgänger of Jesus in the preceding play.[9] Clearly Clare is intended as a Christ figure. In irony she embodies Jesus' Beatitudes: Blessed are the poor in spirit; blessed are they that mourn; blessed are the meek; blessed are the merciful; blessed are the pure in heart; blessed are the peacemakers; blessed are they which are persecuted (Matthew 5). She is the Good Shepherd who knows her sheep and they her, who calls them by name, who has joy at finding the one lost, and who will lay down her life for them. Doomed to an April crucifixion, she is forsaken, has no place to lay her head, is ridiculed and rejected by man. For Jeffers, her "impurity" is her desire to save others from pain. Obsessed with the welfare of her sheep, she only succeeds in losing them — to man's thoughtless cruelty or to a Darwinian nature.

9. Rolfe Humphries in the *New Republic* for April 9, 1930, speculates that Jeffers was inspired by George Moore's *The Brook Kerith,* the *Dear Judas* being offspring of the first part, *The Loving Shepherdess* coming from Moore's depiction of Jesus' idyllic life after sequestering by the Essenes following the crucifixion. For parallels to Sir Walter Scott's Madge Wildfire in *The Heart of Midlothian,* and especially to Scott's source, Feckless Fannie, a legendary shepherdess who wandered England and Scotland attended by a small flock, see Fraser Drew, "The Loving Shepherdess of Jeffers and Scott," *Trace* (April-May, 1959), 13–16.

The story's structure is episodic, a string of incidents along a mystical journey north,[10] which constitutes a symbolic thrust toward the Center, Night, God, and Annihilation. Clare is Everyman, a kind of ragbag that could be either male or female (p. 50). She is the mystic fool, mad by all socio-psychological criteria, yet somehow more than just insane. Her journey northward lies along a sky range, the route of ancient migrations, to the "appointed high place," to a promised land, to nowhere. It is a passage through perils from man, beast, and elements; it is a trial, a labyrinth, a quest, a return to the womb. Clare is scapegoat; her drama has titanic dimensions; she re-enacts the ancient autumnal rites of cycle-end in which the old king must yield his life and world to the new.

Clare herself, gentle and undemanding, self-sacrificing, totally altruistic, a woman and a mother, seems the perfect vehicle by which definitively to test the savior impulse. Jeffers begins his story *in medias res*. Clare's lover has

10. Jeffers provides twelve numbered divisions to his text (the captions are added):

I   Schoolhouse Harassment
II   River, Dream, and Folger's Kindness
III Point Sur Beach and Will Brighton
IV   Sur Hill and Onorio
V   Onorio on Visions
VI   Little Sur Canyon: the Warfields
VII Mill Creek Farm: Woman-Harried Man
VIII Camp under Bridge: Clare's Story
IX   Clare's Story
X   Clare's Protectiveness
XI   Onorio's Visions and Clare's Dream
XII Salmon Run and Clare's Death

The incidents along the way of Clare's journey — the children, Folger, Will Brighton, Warfield and sons, the hired man, the woman-harried farmer, and Vasquez — whether intentional or not, read like personifications of the seven deadly sins: pride, covetousness, lust, anger (hatred), gluttony, envy, and sloth.

killed her father; she has lost her first child in a fever after her trial; she has left her father's ranch when shipwreck refugees threaten her flock. Pregnant again by one who befriends her, she has begun a distracted, lonely, compulsive hegira, ostensibly to save her sheep but more and more clearly to walk a fated *via dolorosa*. We find her in manic-depressive moods, weeping uncontrollably before the certainty of her end or giggling contentedly over her sheep. She is driven on irrationally, almost a sleepwalker, refusing what sparse help is offered. She will take care of the needy till she dies. She tells Onorio that she feels that pain is from "restraint of love"; therefore she loves all, gathers all, will leave glad memories for all. She rejects suicide and abortion, yet is ignorant of the Caesarean section that might save her. She has broken out of humanity but not sufficiently. She sentimentalizes; she mothers all things: child, sheep, and universe. She must finally be purified by yielding her attachment and her savior delusion.

Jeffers' scene is the landscape of the lonely, rugged, precipitous, inhospitable coast that hangs from the base of the Coast Range between Big Sur and Carmel. It is the so-called "Jeffers Country," which not only served as locus and backdrop for his stories but constituted chief protagonist.[11] The difference is that Clare's story seems to subsume the others. As she passes the landmarks found in earlier narratives, Jeffers attaches to them the names of the previous agonists — Barclay's (Point Sur), Cawdor's (Bixby Landing and Rocky Creek), Cauldwell's (Point Lobos).

Typically Jeffers' flora — sorrel, lavender, cresses, lu-

11. See "My Loved Subject" in *The Beginning and the End* (New York, 1963), p. 50.

pine, yucca, jealousy, maidenhair, redwood sorrel, colts-
foot, wake-robin, yellow violet, Solomon's seal, etc. — are
the wildflowers and associated vegetation of the coast from
Sur to Carmel Valley. They are also characteristic re-
minders of the cycle-end and of the year-god's annual
sacrificial death. The fauna — animals, birds, and fish —
partake also of this double image, being both realistic
coastal wildlife and reminders of the rituals of death and
renewal. The archetypal lamb or sheep becomes the lion's
victim. The heron, thrice-falling prey of the merciless
hawk, is an obvious Christ/passion symbol. The salmon,
at the end of Clare's journey, re-enact a yearly sacrificial
ritual which Jeffers describes so stunningly in his lyric
"Salmon-Fishing." The continuing typological references
— Vicente Springs, Sur River, Point Sur, Sur Hill, Little
Sur River, Serra Hill, Mescal Creek, Mill Creek Canyon,
Sovranes Reef, Carmel Valley — move us accurately up
the map. They also reinforce the step-by-step inevitability
of the journey. Seasonal references, color patterns, imag-
ery of music, war, death, and dark — all work together to
depict the truth Jeffers is everywhere seeking to drama-
tize: the monomyth and cyclic ritual of eternal return, to-
gether with concurrent themes of determinism, delusion of
efficacy, amorality of pain, and reconciliation of evil.

Clare pursues her fatal course up this California coast
from well below Big Sur to the San Joaquin Valley. Her
driving determinism is more evident in the final phase, as
it is psychologically inexplicable. Her flock of sheep has
dwindled from hundreds to a pitiful few and finally to
none. North proves the way to bitter Calvary and darkness.
In a key passage, the poet interjects:

Unhappy shepherdess,
Numbed feet and hands and the face

Turbid with fever:
You love, and that is no unhappy fate,
Not one person but all, does it warm your winter?
Walking with numbed and cut feet
Along the last ridge of migration
On the last coast above the not-to-be-colonized
Ocean, across the streams of the people
Drawing a faint pilgrimage
As if you were drawing a line at the end of the world
Under the columns of ancestral figures:
So many generations in Asia,
So many in Europe, so many in America:
To sum the whole. Poor Clare Walker, she already
Imagines that sum she will cast in April [pp. 80–81].

April is the month of death and resurrection, the season of
Christ's passion. Clare will die in an agony of obstructed
childbirth. The "sum" will be pain and death. Symbolically
Jeffers projects in her the fate of Western civilization, if
not the race of men — in final apocalypse, dying of its own
mystic misapprehensions and of the inevitability fatally
present in all things that live or die.

This apocalyptic dimension is characteristic of Jeffers'
narratives.[12] Somehow the fate of mankind and of the
globed earth is foreshadowed and implicated in the little
lives so grotesquely thwarted. Tamar's holocaust is at-
tended by torchbearing spectral armies of World War I,
and it takes place on the "drop-off cliff of the world" which
in David's fantasy overlooks "the ocean boiling and the

12. See "Apocalyptic Dimension of Jeffers' Narratives," *Robin-
son Jeffers Newsletter*, no. 32 (July, 1972), 4–7. Actually this
apocalyptic dimension is present throughout *The Loving Shep-
herdess* in the titanic suggestion given the landscape and pro-
tagonist in such phrases as "storms racing below us," "the world's
sag-end," "dark immense lines going out of the world," "burnt on
the gable of the world with near sun and all winds."

sea curl[ing] up like paper in a fire and the dry bed crack[ing] to the bottom." In *Roan Stallion,* the final sacrificial death takes place within a child's vision of world deluge. In *The Tower Beyond Tragedy,* Cassandra sees the play's action taking place in a "world cataractlike [which pours] screaming onto steep ruins." Elsewhere she pictures the same earth, stage for human delusions of stability and power, as changing poles, staggering, reeling, and whirling. *Thurso's Landing* locates the protagonists on the prow of a ship (civilization) that, in "the coming time," is to strike, founder, and go down. In these and other instances, civilization's demise is precipitated by dramatic elemental cataclysms — fire, quake, storm, flood. In *The Loving Shepherdess,* the world of westering man ends in mindless self-sacrifice and in the inability to give birth. Jeffers may be anticipating here what he will later speculate on in his foreword to *At the Birth of an Age* — that the Christian age, a hybrid of Attila-like ruthless energies and passive Christian self-sacrifice, is coming to its close in a "long decline," characterized by a reduction of Christian faith into "generalized philanthropy, liberalism, socialism, communism, and so forth."[13] Jeffers saw Christian saviorism transmuted into many secular forms.

Key to the poem's denunciation of this savior syndrome is the vision sequence shared by Onorio with Clare (pp. 103–107). It begins with a spectral procession of Indian migrations from Asia to Aztec and Mayan Central America. This is the most ancient element of the racial amalgam finalized on the Pacific shore and personified in Onorio himself. The vision seems to founder a moment in a digression on imperial power and pretentious human science. These megalomanias are soon reduced to absurdity in the

13. *Selected Poetry,* p. 505.

context of a dust-grain earth in a flip-penny galaxy within a spendthrift cosmos. Onorio's vision gains the final full dimension which, for Jeffers, alone gives all things their value and reality — the universe as a whole. Here Onorio experiences the homogeneity of the stars and atoms, the pulsating energy-life that fills every cranny. He sees it all reducible to "the eye that makes its own light and sees nothing but itself" (Jeffers' self-torturing, pantheistic god). The vision constitutes an overwhelming reconciliation of opposites in which saviorism becomes preposterous.

Clare's dream coincides with this mystically reductive vision in which all energy and life are merged. She too has seen the whole universe "blended into one tiny light." The vision is true but neither Clare nor Vasquez is able to embrace it wholly. Onorio's mind short-circuits; Clare's sentimentalizes. They are told a saving truth: "Good and evil balance perfectly; there is no glad or sorry"; "The great river of the blood of life is always bursting its banks, never runs dry." But they do not heed; they do not let go. Clare would comfort the "fire-studded egg of heaven," cuddle it, save it from harm as she would her sheep. She would return it to her womb for an idyllic life which she has decreed for her own child (pp. 102–103); thereby she denies life. In Jeffers' metaphysics there is no vitality except by violence. To prevent pain, to resist life and death, is to deny God. This is the purport of Onorio's final vision on the road (p. 112). In legend, Peter the apostle, fleeing persecution in the imperial city, asked a spectral Christ, "Quo vadis?" which is to say, "Where are you going?" and was answered, "To Rome to be crucified." Vasquez meets a similar vision, who protests, "If I go up to Calvary ten millions times: what is that to you? Let me go up." This Christ is the antinomy of saviorism; he is the year-

[*149*]

god victim perennially repudiating the shepherd syndrome.

Jeffers here sets two perceptions of reality against each other: Clare's perception of her protective role is contrasted with an overview perception embodied in this vision sequence which closes with Christ's final denial of the savior role classically attributed to him. The vision, painfully ignored by the two participants, is corroborated by the nature dramas of the heron and the salmon, which reiterate that all is fated, pain is no evil, saviorism is a human illusion, nothing in the world's life process can be changed. Clare herself demonstrates this merciless but beautiful inevitability all the while she is denying it.

The story's ending is enigmatic. Epiphany and catharsis are to be had by the reader, rarely by the protagonists, in Jeffers' stories. Tamar, Orestes, Cawdor — a very few are so privileged. In the final scene by the San Joaquin River, under a thin April rain, along a road whose poplars "reach dreadfully away northward," Clare is overtaken by labor pains. "In the evening, between the rapid/ Summits of agony before exhaustion, she called/ The sheep about her and perceived that none came." Does she suffer a final clarity? "Perceived" is a word unusual for Jeffers. He uses it three times in this poem: on an earlier occasion it was chosen to distinguish from "imagined" when specifying Onorio's vision of cosmic oneness and balance (p. 108); later, just before the apparition of Christ, it describes Vasquez's discernment that Clare will go on to her end despite anything he does. Possibly, then, Jeffers' most sympathetic protagonist, this gentle girl who has won the hearts of many critics who are generally put off by Jeffers' creations, is allowed momentarily to transcend the ironic parable that she embodies. As Jeffers' heroes and heroines go, she has already progressed far along the road to clarity and unstigmatized vision. She is, as he attests, a "saint," a "natural martyr," embodying love "undefiled." If she herself can here finally recognize that love as "inefficient," she thereby becomes one with Christ going to Calvary ten million times — without reservations about the painful but true conditions of being. She becomes a willing participant in the sacrificial flood of the "great river of the blood of life," who can worship wholly, free from the subtle arrogance that desires to change God's will and alter the nature of life, one who can finally contemplate the "fire-studded egg of heaven" without needing to save it or any of its parts.

Of the remaining poems here collected, no extended commentary seems called for. Having been published earlier in various magazines, they may seem less specifically written for this volume, which appears to be complete in the interplay of the Judas and Shepherdess dramas. However, they do elaborate on the Inhumanist proposition inherent in those stories.[14] "The Humanist's Tragedy," the third narrative, is one of Jeffers' shortest and most condensed. It recapitulates Euripides' *The Bacchae* to illustrate a favorite Jeffers theme: the danger and doom involved in the human megalomania. Thebes' King Pentheus, the Apollonian embodiment of reason, human hegemony, and centrality, is destroyed for his arrogance and

14. "Inhumanism" as an articulated philosophical stance was not publicly espoused by Jeffers until 1948 in his now famous Preface to *The Double Axe*, where it is defined as "a shifting... from man to not-man; the rejection of human solipsism and recognition of the transhuman magnificence." "It offers," he says, "a reasonable detachment as rule of conduct, instead of love, hate and envy. It neutralizes fanaticism and wild hopes; but it provides magnificence for the religious instinct, and satisfies our need to admire greatness and rejoice in beauty."

presumption, being torn apart by Agave, his mother, and the whole band of Dionysus' devotees whose forest mysteries he has so irreverently broken in upon. The story is a parable of Inhumanism, a warning against the human delusion of control. It scores again the errant saviorism variously manifested in *Dear Judas* and *The Loving Shepherdess*.

"The Broken Balance," an example of Jeffers' long, meditative, philosophical poems, provides the prophet-poet and his reader with a reconciliation to the cleansing disaster coming to civilization. The "balance" here is the crest of the culture wave; "broken" anticipates the downward fall, the shattering and diminution. Structured loosely on a six-part division, the poem gives witness to signs that the present age is passing, and it ponders the relative values of sickly conformity and of revolutionary power. After contrasting men with the more honest animals and urging that the earth be mercifully eased of man's presence, Jeffers ends with a reluctant palinode, a partial retraction, admitting that there may be a redeeming beauty even in man.

"Birth-Dues" is a pivotal Jeffers lyric. In it the poet deals with his debt to the human race. Having dissociated himself so often and abhorred the race's egomania and other perversions, he pauses to reconsider his residual responsibility. He is a man; he must speak to men. The poem attempts to epitomize the wisdom that might save the race. Abjure joy and pleasure, he says, for they are trifling. Value pain, harbinger of real values. Know the inhuman self-torturing god; there is no other and he will purify your yearnings. Be prepared to seem monstrous to others.

Lacking totally the usual recriminations, "Evening Ebb"

is a picture without sound: diminished surf, dusk colors, and the planet Venus in its evening epiphany. "Hands" meditates on an archeological discovery in Tassajara, sixty or so miles south of Carmel, a cave in which ancient peoples left impressions of their humanity — which Jeffers reads as gestures of brotherhood and warnings of extinction. "Hooded Night" re-creates the world toward dawn, ocean winds bringing fog, ancient rock and trees looming from the dark. The poet notes "here is reality," antedating man, presently ignoring him as a mere "spectral episode," and enduring godlike. It is a fitting close to the volume.

California State University　　　Robert J. Brophy
Long Beach

TEXTUAL NOTE

Abbreviations

LT   Liveright text, 1929. Whenever double page numbers appear, they refer to manuscript and Liveright pages in that order.

MS   Manuscript, Beinecke Library, Yale University

DJ   The play *Dear Judas*

LS   The narrative *The Loving Shepherdess*

Dear Judas

The *Dear Judas* manuscript consists of forty-two numbered sheets of $8\frac{1}{2} \times 11$–inch white paper, the holograph being written in pencil on one side of the sheets for the most part. The first three leaves are outsize scraps from two torn envelopes. The published text is forty pages in all. The manuscript went originally to John Hay Whitney with a cover letter by Jeffers saying that the poem was written in 1928. This manuscript is now in the Collection of American Literature, Beinecke Rare Book and Manuscript Library, Yale University. Search for typescript and galley proofs has proved futile.

The manuscript opens with a preamble and/or set of notes later abandoned. The fragments are separated by penciled lines across the page. Some are further compartmentalized by vertical lines.

We alone and one other, still shelled in the compressed passion of our living, walk in the moonlight, [two undecipherable words] shadows unravelling the threads of passion.

Gethsemane
These cypresses though twisted by centuries
Are not the cypresses

Are you there again, Judas? (After the kiss). Oh Judas, these torches and those voices are imaginary. Kiss me, as always.

Mary, the [undecipherable] old woman remembering *her* sin.

He explains Judas to himself and sets him free, then Mary, the maniacal singer of self-accusation and curses and wild praise of her son's name in the world; he explains and sets free; he himself is not free till the end of the world. "I have saved others, myself I cannot save."

He asks Mary: "Who was my father?" She answers like a madwoman, still concealing her sin, "The giant stone by the road below Bethlehem."

He understands that he chose God for his father because he did not know who his father was; yet he knows that he actually became God in moments; at those moments he was the origin and approver of evil as well as good. Evil was as beautiful as good; yet he hates evil, how can that be? He returns to the crucifixion of his mind.

The first fragment indicates the Noh character of the drama. The second emphasizes the two thousand years of continuing dynamism — as though Jesus' passion will not burn out till his grip on history is loosed. The third fragment tries a way into the action which is unremitting cycle; the fourth notes Mary's myopia and petty fixation as contrasted with Jesus' grandiose and calculated act. The fifth fragment seems a tentative plot direction which was never carried through; for Judas is never set free, nor is Mary. The quotation from Luke 23:35 adapts the scoffers' words below the cross to bespeak Jesus' own self-evaluation. It emphasizes the magnitude and intensity of his passion (the other passions in comparison are quite personal, fitful, and narrow). Jesus comes close to exemplifying the rationale theologians give for eternal damnation — a free, willful choosing of "evil," which is a self-definition and a fundamental interior reorientation. What Jesus commits is a form of the "unforgivable sin"; he is like a fallen angel, incapable of remorse or change of heart. This suggests that his condemnation may be indeed "till the end of the world" instead of merely till the end of the Christian age.

After this interesting set of fragments, the text as Jeffers published it begins in midpage of the first manuscript sheet. The title, "Dear Judas," is printed large in capital letters and underlined. There follows a note: "See first two lines over next page," which directs to the preamble that he finally decided on. Verse three then begins the dialogue, with the person speaking (here Jesus) typically underlined.

The first ten verses (the first page of both manuscript and final text) show twenty-one corrections in the form of cancellations and additions. The next ten verses, constituting page 2 of the manuscript, reveal seven changes; page 3 allows only three minor alterations. From this point on, the pattern seems to be deletions of from one to five lines every three or four pages but few, very minor changes otherwise.

Occasionally Jeffers inserts sections written on an added page (e.g., p. $11\frac{1}{2}$ and its verso, containing some twenty-three verses) or scribbled on the back of the manuscript page (see pp. 2, 24, 32, 41), the insertion point and section to be added being indicated by the mark ⊗. The page numbering is Jeffers' own.

When correcting, the poet typically lines out the word or phrase and writes above it. Infrequently he writes over words. When a word or phrase is to be added, which is frequent enough, he uses the mark ∧. Occasionally a decision to reverse word position is indicated by the usual proofreader's sign ∾. Reinstatement of canceled words and phrases is designated by a broken underline. Italics are directed by a line under the word.

From the first writing, the poet runs his verse to whatever its desired length by additional half lines or by a series of half lines. His paragraphing is decisive from the beginning.

Jeffers' handwriting is extremely illegible, the letters being flattened out in each word to a mere wavy line. The comparison of manuscript and text would have been a monumental and perhaps impossible task had not Jeffers adhered almost entirely to his original word and line choices. Thus the editor finds himself saying, "Ah, so that's what that word is; I would never have known, but I can see it after the printed text tells me what it is." One turns each page with the apprehension that Jeffers might have decided to rewrite while in the process of doing his typescript; deciphering the original choice of wording would then become a serious obstacle.

Once completed, with changes and corrections, the manuscript text was copied almost word for word by Jeffers; there evidently were few changes from manuscript to typescript. The first three manuscript pages, for instance, show exact equivalence with the published text except for the addition of an adverb to a stage direction. The first ten pages reveal only thirteen minor changes: the substitution of a word, a rephrasing, the addition of a few words, and the reconstruction of a line by dropping a phrase in one place and adding one in another part of the line.

In a few instances the "corrections" from manuscript to final text seem to be mistakes in transcription. "Bright abortions," for instance, on page 16 becomes the less comprehensible "right abortions." Sometimes the new word choice reverses the sense or image, as "happier" for "bitter" birds on page 23.

Except for the changes on page 39, the only instances of Jeffers' rewriting whole lines after the manuscript version was completed occur in the final scene (pp. 45–49) as noted below. To end the play Jeffers added a final verse to the completed manuscript text: "While the white moon glides from this garden; the glory of darkness returns a moment, on the cliffs of dawn." The picture must have seemed structurally useful if not critical, the moon symbolizing the haunted specters caught in their cycle of passion, the darkness representing the momentary lull before the play will begin again.

The following notes remark on the changes from the *Dear Judas* manuscript to the final Liveright text (not revisions in variant printings). They reveal Jeffers characteristically revising minimally after his manuscript version was completed. The italic page and line references at the left are to the Liveright 1929 text, which is reprinted here with only two relatively insignificant corrections. On page

16, line 7, "bright" is restored from the Jeffers manuscript as making more sense than "right." On page 21, line 29, an obvious error in spacing is emended.

10.5 Jeffers adds "abstractedly" after "moving" to further specify a key stage direction

11.24–25 replaces the phrase "For God has told me" with "I have long known you," emphasizing Jesus' perspicacity

11.29 changes "I know not" to the more vernacular "I don't know"

13.23 drops a repeated "What could I think?" before "Not" and adds "against my own source" after "impute" to specifically relate his anguish to the mother's unresolved sin

14.25 replaces "in" with "into"

14.29 substitutes "saving" for "helping"

15.32 replaces "hollow" with "transparent," probably as richer in connotation

15.33 substitutes "line" for the less imaginative "make"

16.7 gives "right" for "bright," probably by an error in transcribing

17.1 replaces an undecipherable word in the MS with "as"

17.14 substitutes "life" for "the earth," thus making Judas' statement more metaphysical

17.16 changes "whipped" to "flogged"

17.17 cancels "endures" for "can endure"

17.28 drops "Creatures" for the less abstract "all that lives"

18.14 replaces "height" with the more concrete and visual "pier"

18.32 rephrases by dropping "and" after "sorrowful"

and adding "are" after "eyes," making the structure more parallel

19.1   adds "ah" before "brittle"

19.16   substitutes "dreadful" for the much used "bitter"

21.7   converts "paving" to "pavement"

21.23   switches "brightness" to "softness," thus altering the visual picture

21.29   leaves an error in spacing: "Wil lhear"

21.30   alters "he'd not" to "he needn't"

23.31   replaces "bitter" with "happier," making more consistent sense

25.6   drops "him" after "follow," making the verb more generally descriptive of the automatism of the crowd

26.5   changes "proudly" to "with pride"

27.24   drops "humbly" after "stands," perhaps wishing Mary to appear more enigmatic

28.10   adds the stage direction "He stands rapt in thought"

28.18   drops "shrunk" for "dwindled"

29.4   makes stage direction more specific by adding "on the right" after "out"

31.14   rewrites "meant as betrayal" into "means to betray me" as more concrete

33.13   reinstates "their cruelty sublimed" after crossing it out in the MS

33.14   interjects "I think" between "and" and "the brute cross"

33.31   substitutes "coming" and "approaching" for "having come" and "approached"

34.9   changes "dares" to "dare," judging "handful" to be plural

34.15   drops *"arrest* you:" after "to" as superfluous

34.24   supplies "force" for "push"

35.30 drops "for" before "now" and adds "that" after it, thus changing the clause from a cause to a concession

36.10 drops "that's your vocation" after "them," perhaps as too distracting and too defining

37.6 converts "that's plenty" to the more scripturally flavored "it's enough"

37.16 replaces "the world breaks" with "the north moves"

39.12 mutes "God" to "his glory," thus conforming to scriptural restraint

39.15 changes "followers" to "companions," perhaps reflecting that they have just experienced the definitive eating of bread together (Last Supper); "as the torches surround him" is then added, giving their location in Gethsemane

39.19 substitutes the next four verses (from "And cut" to "Tell them so, Judas") for the verse "And felled an ear, but fight, fight! Poor braggart, so tamely?"

39.23 changes "they" to "his companions"

45.14 drops an illegible word for "sickness"

45.17 changes "entering" to "Judas enters," making the participial phrase a sentence and full stage direction

45.19 substitutes "telling" for "snapping," which adds the connotation of counting the reasons off

45.21 replaces "telling" with "snapping"

45.26 drops "My life's light can ... dying" after "him"

45.27 omits "I ... Ah! Ah ... I ..." before "Money"

45.30 substitutes "to" for "at"

45.32 replaces "fellow" with "friend," echoing Jesus' word as the betrayal began

45.33 substitutes "person" for "fellow," adds "that did it," and drops "I'm not the traitor, I'm not the ..." between "person" and "that"

46.1 replaces "meeting" with "to" in the stage direction

46.6 alters "this's" to "that means"

46.7 converts "fellow" to "person" and drops "best ... his" after "his"

46.8 drops "old" before "Bluebottle"

46.9 omits a second ",oh" after Oh!"

46.9–10 alters "woman's/ The" to "woman/ Is the"

46.12 adds "the skirt of" before "her garment"

46.13 inserts ",mother" after "him"

46.26 omits "(screaming)" after "liars"

46.29 replaces "and then" with "Because you," making the clause causal instead of sequential

46.30 adds "here" before "at your feet"

46.30a drops a stage direction "(the mutes have gathered about them and indicate assent)"

46.32 inserts "Looking up" before "triumphantly"

47.6–7 after "pity" drops "Stop? all my heart at one stroke. I couldn't endure the anguish/ The sun shines on. But this can't ... I never imagined him condemned ..." and adds "Wasn't that ... No.No."

47.12 replaces "that I'll curse you, Judas" with "I'll be troubled for that?"

47.16 after "In melted iron?" drops "set spear-headed worms in the live entrails to wind outward and pierce/ The shuddering and hateful skin while it crawls, and arch[?] the pink-ringed loops of their flesh and [undecipherable] and reenter?/ I think if I should pray God against you he'd do it."

47.23 replaces "clogged with worse" with "worse fellows"

48.2 substitutes "The Roman Caesar" for "Cold Caesar in Rome"

48.6 changes "ocean-ends" to "ocean ends"

48.8 substitutes "It was bitter ... find him" for "What is this to me? I will go and find him. It may be he has not died but still hangs in torment"

48.11 changes "away" to "off"

48.13 changes "go" to "run"

48.20 substitutes "for many centuries: you" for "while memory retains them you'll"

48.21 converts "eagle's vermin with the eagle" to "hawk's lice with the hawk"

48.23 changes "azure spires" to "blue towers"

48.27 alters "Go and buy one, blue-face" to read "Find one for yourself, Lazarus"

48.28 substitutes "cruelest" for "most cruel"

48.30 after "buy" inserts "myself" to replace "for myself" located after "peace"

48.32 supplants "bitter" with "useless"

49.3 replaces "Jesus in" with "the other at"

49.6–7 added after the manuscript was completed: "While the white moon glides from this garden; the glory of darkness returns a moment, on the cliffs of dawn."

The Loving Shepherdess

Sixty-four numbered sheets of $8\frac{1}{2} \times 11$–inch white paper, written on in pencil, make up the LS manuscript which was sent to John Hay Whitney with a covering letter by Jeffers noting that "'The Loving Shepherdess' was written early in 1929." The manuscript is now at Yale's Beinecke Library. No typescript or galley proof has yet been recovered.

There are fewer changes within the manuscript than in that of *Dear Judas*. Interpolations are infrequent; two or three verses were added on the verso of manuscript pages 7, 28, 31, 41, and 63. About once every page, a line is crossed out; at times three or four verses are deleted. Jeffers occasionally reverses the sequence of words in a line for better effect, as from "rose the sun" to "the sun rose" on manuscript page 58. Two or three times Jeffers rewords a whole phrase or drops a phrase. Several times each page he might change words (from manuscript to typescript), but the changes are minor — "little" to "tiny," "splashing" to "wading," "shepherdess" to "mistress," etc. In one instance a clearer reading seems lost when on LT page 69 "drooping" is substituted for the original "dropping" — probably a slip in transcribing which was never thereafter caught.

The poet divides his text into twelve sections marked by Roman numerals. The placement of these divisions is reconsidered several times (see manuscript pages 13, 21, 29). Jeffers emphasizes periods with an $\times$ mark. Intermittently he reinstates what he has crossed out, indicating this intention with an interrupted underlining of the word or phrase.

His punctuation is consistently unchanged from his first choice in the manuscript to the final printed text. There are few instances of later changes in hyphenation, substitution of semicolon for comma, or providing punctuation previously omitted. Jeffers added a number of ¶ marks to the text (e.g., manuscript pages 42, 45, 49, 56); he does not, however, always follow his own paragraphing (e.g., compare MS page 32 and LT page 82).

The LS manuscript is singularly unremarkable. Again Jeffers' handwriting is quite illegible, the script often flattening out into a wavy line after the initial letter of the word. The only "major" difference of final text from manuscript is an ending of five lines which was dropped entirely:

But Onario Vasquez, on the high coast,
Often watches her pass, against the cloud
On some bare ridge, or against the running stars of
    the sea,

> High-headed, bright-hearted, the sheep huddling about
> her,
> As when they were most happy, to hear her name
> them.

Though these verses are not crossed out, Jeffers evidently thought better of including them, choosing to leave the focus on Clare Walker in her moment of final clarity.

The 1929 Liveright text is reprinted here with only four relatively insignificant corrections. On page 69, line 15, "dropping" is restored as the original Jeffers manuscript choice and as making more sense than "drooping." On page 72, line 17, a period is dropped because it violates the sense and is not to be found in the manuscript. On page 100, line 5, a comma is restored from the manuscript to clarify meaning. On page 104, line 26, a comma is dropped as unnecessary and not to be found in the manuscript.

51.31   Jeffers reinstates "always" after crossing it out in the MS

52.1   replaces "splashing" with "wading"

53.13   substitutes "mistress" for "shepherdess"

54.23   alters "wild-bird" to "wildbird"

54.27   adds "there" after "torn"

58.14   rephrases "rose the sun" to "the sun rose"

59.33   writes "quarters" above "shoulders" in the MS, though "shoulders" is not crossed out

61.30   alters "someone" to "some one"

64.30   replaces "badly" with "wretchedly"

65.29   reinstates "the hurt" after crossing it out

66.7   substitutes "seen" for "known," perhaps integrating Clare into the compass of the visions

69.15   allows "drooping" for "dropping," an obvious error

70.14   adds "church" after "San Antonio"

71.1   reinstates "little" after striking it

71.9   drops "and" before "lead" and replaces "is" with "grows"

72.17 adds a period after "jealousy," possibly an error

74.6   reinstates "out" after striking it

76.12 substitutes "little" for "tiny," perhaps as distracting since "Tiny" is the name of one of the sheep

77.32 drops "I" for "I'll," making it less a hesitation than a resolution or promise

78.2   replaces "pranks" with "tricks"

79.9   reinstates "like" after striking it

79.21 between "loneliness" and "locked" drops the phrase, "nothing alive being near her except the sheep," much shortening the line

82.14 indicates in the MS a new paragraph at "In an hour"

82.33 alters "three" to "it"

85.21 changes "the" to "her," probably to avoid confusion

86.25 adds a comma after "head"

87.22 adds a comma after "world"

87.27 reinstates "poisonous" in preference to "venomous," both of which are struck in the MS

88.5   replaces "No nothing-wisher was ever" with "These nothing-wishers of life are never"

88.16 substitutes "It's bitter to be a" for four illegible words

91.16 changes "they" to "he," altering the point of view, which is made to focus on Charlie's habitat rather than the Walkers'

96.22 inserts "brown" for "grey"

98.22 drops "them" and a comma after "much," thus changing "the flock" from appositive to direct object

100.4 replaces "But late in" with "In the midst of," suggesting a harvest moon and demanding victimhood

100.5   drops a comma after "filled," perhaps an error

100.20   replaces "had all died except little Hornie" with "never seemed able to live"

102.26   substitutes "sky" for "stars," probably as more encompassing and as suggesting "Mother Night"

103.9   adds ellipsis marks after "April"

104.2   adds "along" after "the coast"

104.15   supplies "read" for "heard"

104.20   chooses "canceled" over "cancelled"

104.26   adds comma after "name," perhaps an error

106.7   substitutes "our" for "the"

109.14   hyphenates "great-trunked"

109.16   changes a semicolon to a comma after "calling," making the sentence flow more surely

111.3   contracts "he would" to "he'd"

111.26   substitutes "exactly" for "just," possibly to avoid having April make a value judgment on her doom; marks "Ah, no," to precede "How" but evidently reconsiders

113.15   adds "was" after "she," probably as necessary for sentence sense

113.22   drops "steelhead" before "salmon," possibly to give the symbol more universality

113.27   substitutes "wiggle" for "struggle"

114.29   replaces "toward" with "in the"

114.31   ends the story with the focus remaining on Clare's perception of the circumstances of her death, the five remaining manuscript lines being abandoned as noted above.

Shorter Poems

Of the shorter poems in the *Dear Judas* volume, almost the reverse situation is true. Whereas the two long narratives had seen no variant printings but could be compared with their original manuscript text, these poems had appeared in print before their DJ inclusion, but, except for holographs of "Hands" and "Hooded Night" and typescript sections of "The Broken Balance," they offer no manuscript texts for comparison and study.

THE BROKEN BALANCE

This poem appeared as "The Trumpet" in *Poetry* magazine for January, 1928, and in *Poems* (Book Club of California, 1928). The *Dear Judas* version dropped sections III and IV (originally titled "The Machine" and "July 4th by the Ocean") and added new sections III, IV, V, and VI, renumbering the original V ("Grass on the Cliff") to be section VII, untitled. The whereabouts of the holographs and typescripts of sections I to III is unknown. Three unnumbered sheets, the holograph of section IV, were tipped into copies 1, 3, and 4 of the "large-paper" edition of Alberts' *A Bibliography of the Works of Robinson Jeffers* (New York: Random House, 1933). The holograph of section V (titled "Day after To-Morrow" in both holograph and typescript) was last located in a private collector's hands in New York. The typescript of the same section V has made its way to Yale's Beinecke Library. The holograph of section VI, titled "Palinode," was last reported in another collector's hands in New York (see Alberts, *Bibliography*, pp. 57–58). There is no information currently available on the manuscripts of section VII.

115. title   The passage referred to is section VII (Loeb edition, pp. 345–349), in which Plutarch describes the omens by which the "heavenly powers" foreshadowed the harm to be wrought by Marius' fatal sedition: spontaneous combustion of Roman ensigns, ravens devouring their young in the streets, nice gnawing consecrated gold in the temple and eating their young, and the terrifying sound of a trumpet, shrill and dismal, out of a cloudless sky. "The Tuscan men declared the prodigy foretokened a change of conditions and the advent of a new age." Such a change is also marked by a rise in esteem of the art of soothsaying [prophecy] which is needed to interpret "manifest and genuine signs sent forth by the Deity."

115.6–8 Jeffers rewrote two verses, substituting everything from "final" to "Tuscany" for the original phrasing of "The Trumpet," which ran: "bitter a trumpet blast,/ So long and final clamored out of the cloudless blue over Tuscany."

116. sec. II This second section is verbatim from "The Trumpet"

116. secs. II–IV Being unique to this final version of the poem and no manuscripts being currently available, these sections allow no textual comment or comparison

118. sec. V also new in the *Dear Judas* version, but a typescript is available in Yale's Beinecke Library

118.16 changes "submission" to "prostration" after "hopeless"

118.20 drops "Humanity," which began the line, and an undecipherable modifier and "spores" after "fungus"; adds "slime-threads"

118.21 replaces "slime-threads" with "spores"

119.1 supplies "that snuffed" for "extinct" and "virtue" for "quality"

119.3 five illegible words are crossed out above "Not unrequired though monstrous . . ." which is also crossed out for the five-word line that stands

119.4–6 replaces "Death playing redeemer, proclaiming

that even humanity, the bald ape's offspring, was admirable, but at the sad end" with the final version which runs from "So death will flatter" to "admirable"

119. sec. VI   no other printings or any manuscript texts available for comparison

119. sec. VII   substantially the same as section VI of "The Trumpet"

119.17   revised "the house" to read "my windows" in the DJ version

BIRTH-DUES

"Birth-Dues" had previously appeared in *Poetry* for January, 1928, and in *Poems*. The whereabouts of holograph or typescript manuscripts is unknown.

121.3   substituted "the ass follows" for "that leads," as it had stood in both the *Poetry* and *Poems* versions

THE HUMANIST'S TRAGEDY

"The Humanist's Tragedy" had previously appeared in *Poetry* magazine and in *Poems* under the title "The Women on Cythaeron." It is a capsulizing and reworking of the basic Dionysus story as dramatized by Euripides in *The Bacchae*. The poem's two previous printings offer variations:

122.16   replaces "set in a wall" (*Poems*) and "in a blind wall" (*Poetry*) with "in the breast of a wall"

122.24   revises "you saw" (in *Poetry* and *Poems*) to "saw you"

123.14   adds "the" before "slope"

123.19   adds "the" before "God"

125.19   changes "knows" to "might do it"

"Evening Ebb" first appeared in the *Carmelite,* December 12, 1928. The holograph manuscript is in the collection of Ella Winter. Jeffers produced a facsimile of this holograph for the *Carmelite* issue, showing the following emendations:

127.1 substitutes "five night herons" for "and the cormorants"

127.2 changes "drift over" to "fly shorelong"

127.3a crosses out the line "The clouds come from the fog-wall"

127.5 drops "from the weed-clad rock" from the end of the line, following "down"

127.12 replaces "she was dressing" with "rehearsing"

HANDS

"Hands" appeared previously in the *Carmelite,* December, 1928. The holograph manuscript is at Yale, bearing an earlier title, "Cave of Hands."

128.1 replaces "There is" with "Inside" and leaves "narrow," after considering "crooked"

128.3 substitutes "vault of the rock" for "dark rockwall," later dropping "the" before "rock"

128.7 reverses "magic" and "religion"; replaces "now it becomes in the transit of time" with "the division of years," "division" being a final choice over "canyon," which is canceled.

128.10 changes "become" to "are now"

128.10a cancels "Sealed with the hands of the tribe: we also were"

128.11 reverses position of "We also were human" and

"We had hands, not paws," "we had" replacing the earlier "they are"

128.12   changes "cunning" to "cleverer": "cunning" appeared in the *Carmelite* version.

128.13   replaces "land" with "country"; cancels out "and then come down to us," substituting "her beauty, and come down"

Between line 6 and line 7 of the printed versions, the manuscript shows an eighteen-line (twelve-verse) version of the poem which is heavily lined out and crossed over in pencil.

HOODED NIGHT

"Hooded Night" first appeared in the *Carmelite,* December, 1928; its holograph manuscript is at Yale and reveals the following emendations:

129.1   cancels "when" before "all"

129.4   writes "slumbering" above "sleeping" without canceling either

129.6   drops an illegible word before the first "itself"

129.7   writes "huddles" over a word that cannot be recovered

129.9   cancels successively "dances," "twinkles," "shines," and leaves "sparkles," which he then changed to "glances"

129.10a   crosses out a line: "Their old old shadows in the light of the sky"

129.13   cancels "trees" and "cypresses" and then reinstates "trees"

129.14   deletes "that changed [illegible word]" between "planted" and "the year"

129.14a   pencils out a line: "here is a greater and more just peace," "final" being an alternative for "greater"

129.15   considered "Well," for "But"; decided against "a sacred" after "is"; and crossed out "unlaughable" in favor of "unridiculous"

129.16   originally the line read: "The stones were here, and the ocean, and the trees"

129.20   considers "Oh secure wilderness" before deciding on "Here's reality," which became "Here is reality"

129.21a   pencils out a line: "after the [illegible word]-making council's [illegible word] questions are settled"

129.21b   lines out "Nights like this, quiet and questionless:bead[?] the long shore."

129.21c   cancels "Inexhaustible stands the dark glory."

129.21d   deletes "Questions are checked: the dark glory."

The manuscript text of the poem as published is followed by six lines of canceled poetry, couplets separated from each other by penciled lines crossing the page. The first is a repeat of lines 18, 19, and 20. The second reads: "The world '[illegible word] and intuitive man' intruded. The world as it is, for/His intrusion is after all very modest, except on this planet, and here is a [illegible]." The third shows: "The flash of waves breaking; the glimmer of the whitened cormorant rock/ The dark of the [illegible] of the [illegible] granite rocks against the greymist."

Scriptural Passages Echoed and Adapted in Dear Judas

10.1   inversion of Peter's confession in Mt 16:16

11.1   paraphrase of Mt 11:28, "Come to me . . ."

13.20   question of carpenter father, Mt 1:19; 13:55

18.3, 24   fig tree cursed, Mt 21.19

18.9ff.   Jesus' exaltation is, ironically, the cross, Jn 3:14; 8:28; 12:32

18.16   tower of Siloam catastrophe, Lk 13:4

18.30   "what is that to you": phraseology at Cana, Jn 2:4, and final words, Jn 21:22

19.9ff.   possibly an allusion to Jacob's wrestling, Gen 32:24

19.32   born to be king, Mt 2:2; 27:37; Jn 18:37

20.1   nature of kingdom, messianic or political: see Jn 18:33; 19:19 for Pilate's interrogation and the legend over the cross

20.1   with the Father before the foundation of world, Jn 17:24

20.2   ruled the angels, Mt 16:27; 26:53

20.3   to save a lost people, Mt 18:11

20.8   build the throne of David, shepherd the flock: Lk 20:41; Mt 22:41; Lk 1:32; Ps 110:1; Heb 1:13; 10:13; Acts 2:34–35

20.11   colt for triumphal entry, Jn 12:13

20.16ff.   chiliastic vision, Rev 20

21.1   Bethany as center of activity, Mt 21:17; 26:6; Jn 11:7; 12:1

21.4   denunciation of the Pharisees, Mt 3:7; 12:34; 23:33

21.6   stones would shout, Lk 19:39–40

22.32   not a stone on a stone, Mt 24:2

22.32   able to destroy the temple, Mt 26:62; Mk 14:58

23.5   the Father's equal and God, Jn 5:19ff. Jesus never directly and explicitly claims divinity in the Gospels but implicitly does so in his claim "Before Abraham was I AM," which suggests not only prior existence and causality but echoes the secret name of God, YHWH, the tetragrammaton, I AM, Exod 3:14

[*174*]

33.22   lifted up, drawing all men to my feet, Jn 12:32

35.17   necessary for one man to die . . . , Jn 17:14

36.13   I shall draw all men to me, Jn 12:32

36.27   those that do my will are my mother, Mt 12:48

37.26   keep watch for me one hour, Mt 26:40; Mk 14:37

38.18ff.   men will put out their eyes . . . lest faith become impossible . . . and their souls perish: speech pattern from Mt 13:13–15; meaning inverted

39.12   I have *been* his glory, Jn 1:14, effulgence of the godhead

40.13   My soul doth magnify the Lord, Magnificat, Lk 1:46ff.

41.16   high place: mountaintop places of worship, archetypal meeting with God, 1 Kgs 3:2; 12:31; 14:23; 15:14; 2 Kgs 14:4; 15:35; Is 57:15

41.26   joy like a sharp sword: Simeon's prediction, Lk 2:35

41.31   I am Lazarus who lay dead four days, Jn 11:1ff.

42.22   prayer-hearing Lord: very general but perhaps suggested by Jn 14:13; 15:7; 15:10

42.23   a loving God: reminiscent of the first epistle of John

42.29   Hail Mary, chosen for extremes, Lk 1:28, the angel's message

44.28   Truth is the way, Jn 14:6, "corrected" by Jeffers

45.29   silver thrown back, Mt 27:3

46.3   mark on brow, Gen 4:15; Ezek 9:4, Rev 14:9, i.e., special destiny, doom

46.31   when my eyes see it I'll believe it, Jn 20:25

47.21   a child for Moloch, Lev 20:2

48.2   chosen and made his own fate, Jn 10:8

48.26,30   noosed cord to buy peace, Mt 27:5

50.8 her face lighted from inside, like Christ's transfiguration, Mt 17:2

50.13ff. mocked by children: contrast with Elisha, ironic Christ-type, 2 Kgs 2:23–25

51.6ff. Good Shepherd, guards his sheep, calls them by name, Jn 10:1–16

51.15 meek, exemplar of the Beatitudes, Mt 5:3–12

51.25 Good Samaritan, Spanish Indian boy intercepts, Lk 10:33

52.3 little flock, Lk 12:32

5.4 going northward, going up, as in going up to Jerusalem, Mt 20:18

52.16 broken loaf, shared bread with sheep, Mt 14:19; 26:26; note 10 sheep parallel 12 apostles

53.22 sorrow for no reason, like Man of Sorrows, Is 53:3; Mt 26:37

54.7 fate inescapable, Mk 8:31; 9:31; 10:32; Mt 26:39

54.24 does not strike dogs, Mt 12:20; 5:39 (bruised reed and turned cheek)

55.17 doom in April, the Passover time, Mt 26:2

55.31 Folger kneels at her feet, Jn 1:27; Lk 7:38; Mt 26:7; Jn 12:3; 13:5 (the Baptist, the woman at Simon's house, Mary, and Jesus to his disciples)

56.9ff. Clare in the river, light from heavens, Christ or the Baptist, Mt 3:13ff.

57.3 what will you do? shepherd struck, sheep scattered, Mt 9:36

57.4 weeps for sheep as Jesus for Jerusalem, Mt 23:37

59.28 no home, nowhere to lay head, Mt 8:20

63.9 sheep fall into pit, Mt 12:11

66.11 care for needy and go to death, most Christlike, e.g., Jn 10:11; 21:16; 15:13

67.33 hawk and heron, like parable (death is natural, Christ-victimhood), Mt 6:26; 10:31

68.4 heron fisherman, Mk 1:17; Jn 21:6,9 (fishers of men, Christ fisherman)

68.5 labored upward, as in the way of the cross and Mt 20:18

68.17 falls, as at the ritualistic three times in the way of the cross

68.19 love all alike, Mt 5:44

73.4 wheeling swords of the sun, sign of exile at Eden gate, Gen 3:24

73.30 rich man with harvest in barns, like parable, Lk 12:13

77.30 love all people, again as in Mt 5:44; Jn 15:12,17

79.31 gave all bread, as loaves to the five thousand, Mt 14:19

80.10 apocalyptic signs: blood, covered sun, wan light, Mt 24:29

80.26 numbed hands and feet, like stigmata, *via dolorosa* anticipating crucifixion, Jn 20:25

81.7 house of hate, like parable illustrating Mt 5:22

82.7ff. squirrels hide in holes; birds perch; we have no place, Mt 8:20

87.2, 4 bread, stone, symbols reminiscent of Mt 7:9

88.17 two commandments, recall Mt 22:38

89.28 sower figure as in Mt 13:3

95.5 abandoned, alone, Mk 14:50

95.13 forgive me, father, for I didn't know what I was doing, Lk 23:34

95.14 why have you forsaken me, father? Mt 27:46

95.25 watch with me, Mt 26:38ff.

98.2   unable to feed the multitude, Mt 14:19

101.5   Onorio's face like a devil's, perhaps like Judas', Mt 26:14; Lk 22:3

101.23   golden country, calm delight, Eden, Gen 2:8

102.17   after a while you'll remember plainly, Jn 16:4

106.16   burning eye of God, Rev 1:14

106.33   killed and inherited (the kingdom); kill God to be atoned with him (107.3): mysterious phrases suggesting redemption through vicarious sacrifice, Heb 9:15

109.20   rejoices at finding the lost sheep, Mt 18:11ff.; Jn 17:12; 18:9

110.5   river of blood, combining the redemptive powers of river and blood, Mt 14:24; Lk 22:20; Rev 7:14; Jn 7:38; Rev 22:1

112.7   if I go up to Calvary ten million times: what is that to you? as in Christ's rebuke to Peter, Mk 8:33

113.21ff.   another ironic parable from nature, the salmon, which must die to give life and continue the process, Mt 10:31; Jn 12:24 (sparrow and grain of wheat)

113.32   the appointed high place, Mt 20:18; 27:40; Jn 3:14; 8:28; 12:32

114.31,32   summits of agony and perception of abandonment, Mt 26:38, Lk 22:44; Mk 14:50; 15:34